Are South Africans Free?

Also available from Bloomsbury

South Africa, Alexander Johnston
Human Rights and Democracy, Todd Landman

Are South Africans Free?

Lawrence Hamilton

B L O O M S B U R Y

LONDON · NEW DELHI · NEW YORK · SYDNEY

Bloomsbury Academic

An imprint of Bloomsbury Publishing Plc

50 Bedford Square	1385 Broadway
London	New York
WC1B 3DP	NY 10018
UK	USA

www.bloomsbury.com

Bloomsbury is a registered trade mark of Bloomsbury Publishing Plc

First published 2014

British Library Cataloguing-in-Publication Data
A catalogue record for this book is available from the British Library.

ISBN: PB: 978-1-4725-3461-3
HB: 978-1-4725-2693-9
ePDF: 978-1-4725-2888-9
ePub: 978-1-4725-2179-8

Library of Congress Cataloging-in-Publication Data
A catalog record for this book is available from the Library of Congress.

Typeset by Integra Software Services Pvt. Ltd.
Printed and bound in Great Britain

For Lorcan and Cormac
May they live as free South Africans

The truth is we are not yet free; we have merely achieved the freedom to be free, the right not to be oppressed. We have not taken the final step of our journey but the first step on a longer even more difficult road.

Nelson Mandela[1]

This is where politics proper begins: the question is how to push further once the first, exciting wave of change is over, how to take the next step without succumbing to the 'totalitarian' temptation, how to move beyond Mandela without becoming Mugabe.

Slavoj Žižek[2]

[1] N. Mandela, *Long Walk to Freedom* (London: Macdonald Purnell, 1995), p. 617.
[2] S. Žižek, 'Trouble in Paradise: The Global Protest', in *London Review of Books*, 35.14 (18 July 2013), p. 12.

Contents

Acknowledgements

I am very grateful to Mairéad McAuley, Nicola Viegi, Raymond Geuss, Laurence Piper, Peter Vale, Saul Dubow, David James, Christopher Wadman, Ze'ev Emmerich, David Moore, James Furner, Camilla Boisen, Chris Allsobrook, Jérémie Barthas, Carl Knight, Thad Metz, Daryl Glaser, Clive Glaser, David Bilchitz, Ayesha Omar, Nkosinathi Ndlela, Jaeho Kang, Marcos Nobre, Rúrion Melo, Jeremy Jennings, David Plotke, Hannah Winkler, Marta Nunes da Costa and Rae Israel, as well as a number of other colleagues in the Department of Politics, University of Johannesburg, and the Department of Politics and International Studies (POLIS), University of Cambridge, for their comments on earlier versions of this manuscript and their keen interest in these ideas over the years. I am especially indebted to Nicola Viegi, with whom I have researched for some time on representation and public debt in South Africa; without him, Chapter 4 would not have been possible and he has contributed insights to the entire book's argument. I would also like to thank two helpful anonymous Bloomsbury readers and Caroline Wintersgill, my excellent editor there. I am also indebted to various graduate classes and audiences at seminars and conferences at the Centro brasileiro de planejamento (Cebrap) and the Universidade de São Paulo, the University of Johannesburg, the University of the Western Cape, the University of Witwatersrand, Queen Mary University of London, the Universidade do Minho and the University of Cambridge. A big, big thank you also to Ayesha Omar and François Janse van Rensburg for exemplary research assistance over the last few years. All have helped me a great deal in the research and writing of this book, but not all will agree with the outcome and none can be held responsible for any mistakes that may remain; the usual disclaimer therefore holds.

Words cannot express my thanks to Mairéad McAuley for her intellectual and emotional inspiration during the writing of this book. With such balance and love, she managed to retain a semblance of normal life, bring our two little boys into this world *and* complete her own book. This book is dedicated to our boys, Lorcan and Cormac. Besides our input – hardly likely to help – their freer future in South Africa depends on its citizens and political representatives realizing that South Africa still has a long way to go to make all South Africans freer. They are 'born frees', as those that have been born since political liberation (1994) in South Africa are known. One of my most fervent wishes is that they be given a meaningful choice in all of the elections they participate in and real power to determine the economic and political choices of their representatives, something that I have never had. Although I have voted for the ANC ever since 1994, I will not do so in 2014, for some of the reasons laid out in this book. But nor will I vote for any other party: there is no real alternative in South Africa today, for those that either need to be empowered or who believe in the empowerment of all South Africans. Much has been made of the recent rise of new parties in South Africa, the fact that the elections in 2014 will be the first in which the 'born frees' can vote and that these two eventualities, somehow, will combine to threaten the electoral dominance of the ANC. I am sceptical of this claim mainly because, as I argue in this book, South Africa's electoral system and other forms of economic and political representation that still obtain systemically fail to offer any real alternatives for meaningful citizen power. The 'born frees' are unlikely to make much of a difference until there exists a properly competitive selection procedure and different forms of political representation and participation. The 'born frees' will probably either vote as their parents do (or would have) or not vote at all. May our 'born frees', at least, grow up and participate in a much freer South Africa.

I am grateful to Little, Brown Book Group for permission to use a quotation from Nelson Mandela's *Long Walk to Freedom* as the first epigraph to this book, as I am to the *London Review of Books* and to Slavoj Žižek to use a quotation from his piece, 'Trouble in Paradise: The Global Protest' as this book's second epigraph.

It gives me great pleasure also to thank my friends, Angeline Mcunu and Robert Fraser, the former for posing for this book's cover photo and the latter for enhancing my amateur photograph and helping me crawl my way into the digital age of photography.

Introduction

On 27 April 2014 South Africa will celebrate 20 years of freedom and democracy. There is much to celebrate: successfully consigning the tyrannous and abhorrent regime of apartheid into the dustbin of history; the country's relatively peaceful transition to democracy; a 'founding father' on par with the best in the person of Nelson Mandela; civil, political and social rights for all safeguarded within a lauded, liberal constitution; four peaceful, free and fair democratic elections (five if the elections in 2014 follow suit); many years of moderately healthy economic growth; a relatively free media and an actively critical civil society; and the lifting of large swathes of the population out of conditions of extreme poverty.

There is also, however, a great deal that dampens the mood of celebration, at least for those willing to lift their rose-tinted spectacles and stare hard into South Africa's recent history. Here follows a list of a few glaring examples. First, there is the authoritarian and centralizing creep of Thabo Mbeki's rule, and his associated denial regarding the proven link between HIV and AIDS, and the devastating effect of the stalled rollout of antiretroviral drugs on the lives of millions of South Africans. Second, consider the crisis of legitimacy within the African National Congress (ANC) governing party brought about by as-yet unresolved and highly disreputable allegations and counter-allegations between two opposing camps, one headed by Mbeki and the other by Jacob Zuma. Third, South Africa's poverty, inequality, unemployment, education and general quality of life statistics are appalling for a middle-income country. Fourth, then there are the corruption scandals at the highest level of public office, such as the ongoing and repeatedly delayed commission of inquiry into the alleged massive arms deal corruption; 'Inkandlagate', the exorbitant use of public monies on the 'security upgrading' of president Zuma's private residence; and 'Guptagate', the 'cleared' use of the country's most secure military airport to land a jet filled with guests attending a private wedding hosted by a family (the Guptas) with very close personal and business connections to Zuma's family. Fifth, the country is paralysed by weekly, often violent street protests over corruption in general and the very poor delivery of local public services in particular. Sixth, South

Africa has one of the highest rates in the world of sexual violence against women and children outside of a war zone. Seventh, the country has recently experienced two downgrades in sovereign debt, which results in higher interest payments by government (and thus all citizens) in order to service public debt and a severe dip in economic growth, with little prospect of turning this around in the medium-term future. Finally and most infamously in August 2012 police massacred 34 striking miners at Lonmin's platinum mine in Marikana in the mineral-rich North West Province, an event that shocked the world and every South African, especially given its overtones of the infamous 1960 apartheid massacre at Sharpeville. In other words, South Africa cannot claim to have entered democratic adulthood very auspiciously.

I can be forgiven, therefore, for the impudence of asking whether South Africans are free, given these events a full two decades after South Africa's remarkably peaceful demolition of apartheid. South Africans now live in a true republic as opposed to a republic by name alone, a republic that reduced the majority of its population to non-citizens, strangers in their own land, without formal political power and generally impoverished. In 1994 South Africans were granted equal rights to elect their political representatives, to be treated equally before the law and to move, associate, love and worship as they see fit, and in 1996 a new constitution provided firm ground for these rights to be upheld. Marshalling empirical evidence and theoretical innovation, in this book I argue that political liberation and these formal rights are insufficient for real freedom and, amongst other things, the inauspicious events listed above are the consequence of a deep political and economic malaise that can be explained best by reference to the various forms of representation that were instantiated during South Africa's transition to democracy. In order to see that South Africans are not yet free, it is necessary first to ask what we may mean by freedom or liberty, and assess the institutional framework for representative democracy that was chosen before, during and after formal political liberation alongside current social, economic and political conditions.

This requires the elaboration of a more realistic and substantive account of freedom than is the norm in everyday political language and theory. I call this 'freedom as power through representation' or 'freedom as power'. I summarize an argument here that freedom is power under modern conditions within complex polities and economies in the sense that freedom is identified *with* and *as power*, in that it is a combination of my ability to determine what I will do and my power to do it, that is bring it about. In particular, I argue that my freedom is relative to my power to: (a) get what I want, to act or be as I would choose in the absence of either internal or external obstacles or both; (b) determine the government of my political association; (c) develop and exercise my powers and capacities self-reflectively within and against existing norms, expectations and power relations; and (d) determine my social and economic environment via meaningful control over my economic and political representatives. In other words, power is integral to freedom across most of the domains that are significant for individual existence within complex, modern polities.[1] Here I argue more specifically that South Africans lack freedom across all of these dimensions, and that the main causes for this lie in the nature of institutions and economic and political representation that still predominate in South Africa. Moreover, as I argue below and in Chapter 2, it follows that, although some South Africans are freer than others, all South Africans lack freedom as power and thus that South Africans are not yet free. To be even more exact, especially given that I defend a conception of freedom that admits of degrees of freedom, I argue that, although South Africans are freer than they were under apartheid they are a lot less free than they might otherwise have been had they instantiated institutions that enabled freedom as power across all of these four dimensions.

If we view the current conditions in South Africa through these conceptual glasses, we get a very different answer than the one normally given by those who view South Africa through the spectacles of contemporary conceptions of formal freedom and procedural definitions of democratic rights. The attainment of political freedom, and the formal institutionalization of representative democracy, has not produced real freedom as power. The necessary, difficult and courageous steps towards instantiating freedom as power in South Africa have yet to be made. It follows, therefore, that the question that forms the title of this book is vital and important: if we do not ask it, and ask it correctly, we are likely to fail to find the motivation to achieve the goals for which so many fought and laid down their lives in overcoming colonialism and apartheid. If its asking involves impudence and generates discomfort, especially for those currently in positions of power, all the better, for that too is the point of the book's main argument – South African citizen's will only successfully attain and maintain real freedom if they constantly call their political and economic representatives to account.

I argue, in short, that freedom is power through representation across various domains and that, given that South Africa has failed to instantiate the relevant forms of representation, South Africans continue to lack freedom to a

---

[1] For a full theoretical defence of freedom as power, see L. Hamilton, *Freedom Is Power: Liberty Through Political Representation* (Cambridge: Cambridge University Press, 2014).

debilitating degree. The focus, ultimately, is on the following facts: that existing, skewed forms of economic and political representation reproduce the power and interests of elites rather than generate economic opportunity and political power for all; that South Africa's electoral system implements the idea of proportional representation so literally that it undermines rather than instantiates meaningful representation and thus removes any meaningful political agency from ordinary citizens; and that existing macroeconomic policy fails to address the dire conditions of poverty, inequality, unemployment, inadequate education and thus the provision of freedom as power for all South Africans.

Thus, by means of an account of freedom as power and an empirical analysis of existing economic and political conditions, representation and misrepresentation in South Africa, I submit in this book a means of understanding freedom and its lack in South Africa. In order to avoid confusion, however, it is probably a good idea to explicate at the outset here one particular component of the argument. Those who know anything about South Africa's bloody and divided history will be aware of the famous ANC liberation struggle slogan 'Amandla Awethu!' (or 'Power to the People'), which is still an important party political slogan of the ruling ANC party. 'Amandla Awethu' is an isiZulu and isiXhosa phrase adopted by the ANC and its allies as a rallying cry in the resistance against apartheid in South Africa and fight for freedom. The phrase is still associated with struggles for freedom, both by ANC leaders linking the liberation struggle to current challenges and by popular poor people's movements in protest against ANC government policies and poor delivery of basic services such as water, sanitation, housing and so on. What is sadly ironic about the continued use of this slogan by the ANC is that not only has power not been 'given to the people' in that many of them still remain with little or no real power (and thus freedom), but the continued use of a liberation slogan of this kind two decades after political liberation, under conditions of consolidated representative democracy, is a clear sign of the desire of the ANC to claim exclusive representation of 'the people'. It is ironic since it is this trend within the ruling party, enabled by the macro-political structure, in particular the electoral system, that is one of the main determinants of South Africa's *lack* of freedom – the more the ANC attempts to identify itself with the state and the people, the more South Africa slides towards tyranny and the less freedom prevails.

As I shall argue in the second half of the book, given that freedom under modern conditions amounts not so much to the people ruling themselves, but to the representatives of all groups in society having meaningful access to the determination of political and economic policy, any one group of representatives that claims to represent 'the people' is claiming exclusive power and freedom over these processes of policy determination. This is now the case in South Africa, and it is the result of a situation in which the majority party confuses its role as a representative of the majority and its role as representative of the state as a whole (or 'the people'). As a party it *can* claim legitimately to represent a majority of the citizenry (i.e. those who support the ANC), although whether in fact it furthers the interests of the large number of poor and unemployed who support it is debatable. However, as a ruling party in the legislature (and as the executive) it represents the state and the people as a whole. Any confusion of the two, that is, any confusion of the party as a political party competing for power and those members of the party that at any one time represent South Africans, as the sharpest thinkers down the ages have maintained, is a recipe for tyranny or despotic government – hardly good grounds for freedom. So, as I argue in the book's concluding chapter, for power really to be returned to the people and thus for freedom to prevail in South Africa, a number of changes have to be affected: sovereignty returned to parliament; real redistribution of wealth and power amongst the various groups that make up 'the people'; real and meaningful competition to represent these groups; a complete reorganization of South Africa's electoral system that would enable this competition; the introduction of partisan institutions of political participation and legislation for the exclusive representation of the socially and economically least powerful; a decennial constitutional plebiscite; macroeconomic policy directed towards meeting people's needs and overcoming domination (and thus empowering) of all South Africans; competent, courageous, responsible and persuasive leaders; and a restructuring of the ruling alliance.

Representation is a tricky art in representative democracies and the identification of the representatives with the represented spells the end of representation and thus the end of democratic politics and the possibility for freedom. Another way of putting this, as I argue in Chapter 3, is that representation in all senses, in art, theatre, law, economics, politics and so on, depends upon the maintenance of a 'gap' between the object being represented and the representation itself. In politics, this means rigorous individual and institutional means to create and maintain a 'gap' between the citizens, groups thereof, the people or the state on the one side and the representatives on the other. The smaller this 'gap', the lesser the freedom obtained. South Africa is not yet free because, despite large formal and highly lauded transformational processes such as the Constitution of 1996 and the Truth and Reconciliation Commission, the cosy relation between capital and state remains as firm as ever. (Though, as elaborated upon in Chapter 3, the irony is that this is not the case in the requisite *formal* sense – the representatives of capital in general are not deemed to enjoy a veto point in South Africa's formal institutions of representative democracy – and so South Africa is still deemed a risky place in which to invest.)

The form of crony capitalism that characterized the apartheid era has, if anything, been strengthened. In other words, the lack of 'gap' between certain powerful groups of citizens and their formal political representatives that existed under apartheid has not changed. Some of the faces may have changed, but the country is still run by a small economic and political elite that, more often than not, overlaps; that is, the power relations that exist between a set of informal economic representatives and the country's formal political representatives are the major determining factor in South Africa's lack of freedom. Many of the new entrants to the economic elite are high-ranking ANC members, thanks to the policies of Black Economic Empowerment (BEE) and even Broad-Based Black Economic Empowerment (BBBEE)[2]; and those that are not (normally from the old 'white' economic elite or an emerging 'black' economic elite) have direct and powerful links to the new political representatives either as a consequence of being involved themselves in the transition to democratic rule or as a result of being willingly co-opted by political power since the end of apartheid.

A quick note on racial terminology before proceeding: the apartheid era categorizations of 'black', 'indian', 'coloured' and 'white' are still in use today, which explains why in some instances I have no choice but to use them; but when I do I keep them in scare quotes for, as will become clear, I think this fact is very unfortunate.[3]

The lack of 'gap' introduced above and discussed in detail in Chapter 3 is being tragically played out beyond all reasonable doubt by, and as a consequence of, the August 2012 massacre by police of miners at Lonmin's platinum mine in Marikana and the fact that at least one high-ranking Lonmin board member, Cyril Ramaphosa, once union leader, turned very wealthy businessman, with impeccable ANC struggle credentials and with direct links to the highest seats of political power, allegedly exacerbated an already-tense situation by suggesting that the cause of the initial unrest was nothing less than criminal and therefore

---

[2] A. Butler, 'Black Economic Empowerment since 1994: Diverse Hopes and Differentially Fulfilled Aspirations', in I. Shapiro and K. Tebeau (eds), *After Apartheid: Reinventing South Africa?* (Charlottesville: University of Virginia Press, 2011), pp. 52–71.

[3] For more on why, see 'Theorising Race: Imaging Possibilities', *Theoria: A Journal of Social and Polticial Theory*, 136 (September 2013), guest edited by K. Erwin and G. Maré, including their introduction and four cutting edge papers.

required a firm, 'concomitant' response.[4] Despite differences of opinion and speculation, the press rendered this as the fall of a great hero, but, if the main argument of this book is correct, Ramaphosa's situation is the symptom of a broader institutional malaise: the forms of representation and power that exist within contemporary South Africa generate not freedom but tyranny and tyranny breeds this kind of tragic folly. The major difference between Ramaphosa and other ANC cadres is that he was one of the main architects of these very institutions, in particular the constitution, the centrepiece in a legal, political and economic structure that, as I argue, will not produce freedom unless it is radically reformed. I qualify these claims with 'allegedly' because, as I write these lines, the commission into the massacre is still ongoing and Ramaphosa, now Deputy President of the ANC, is now in a position that may ensure that he emerges more or less untainted or at least unscathed.

The other reason I feel justified in asking whether South Africans are free is because, as this book's first epigraph enunciates, one of Africa's greatest and most experienced freedom fighters, Nelson Mandela, was quick to warn his fellow, recently liberated citizens that real freedom was not equivalent to liberation from alien rule. The overthrow of colonialism and apartheid was only the first step on the long road to freedom. In other words, he warned against the complacency of simply assuming that freedom would follow directly and simply from political liberation. Just a little over 20 years after Mandela articulated his warning, literally on the day I write these lines, South Africa and the world mourn the death of Mandela, 'The Father of the Nation', as he is so often called. You might say that he is, for most South Africans, the original virtuous 'Lawgiver', to use a term with ancient roots but made famous by, amongst others, Niccolò Machiavelli and Jean-Jacques Rousseau.[5] Mandela was the guiding light of a peaceful transition to a new, democratic polity with the judgement and humility to step away from power once the nascent state had begun to find its feet. Mandela's caution that the attainment of political

---

[4] D. Smith, 'Lonmin emails Paint ANC elder as a Born-again Robber Baron', *The Guardian*, 24 October 2012, Available from: www.guardian.co.uk/world/2012/oct/2/lonmin-emails-anc-elder-baron [Accessed 25 October 2012]; R. Munusamy, 'Cyril Ramaphosa: Betrayal Does Not Get More Painful Than This', *The Guardian*, 25 October 2012, Available from: www.guardian.co.uk/world/2012/oct/25/cyril-ramaphosa-marikana-email [Accessed 25 October 2012]; Business Day, 'Ramaphosa may Have Fallen Victim to Political Manoeuvre', *Business Day*, 25 October 2012, Available from: www.bdlive.co.za/blogs/politics/2012/10/25/ramaphosa-may-have-fallen-victim-to-a-political-manoeuvre [Accessed 25 October 2012].

[5] N. Machiavelli, *The Discourses*, ed. B. Crick, trans. by L. J. Walker with revisions by B. Richardson (London: Penguin, 2003 [ca. 1517]); J-J. Rousseau, *The Social Contract*, in Rousseau, *The Social Contract and other later political writings*, ed. V. Gourevitch (Cambridge: Cambridge University Press, 1997 [1762]).

freedom from oppression and tyranny is merely the first step on a long journey towards freedom came alongside another, oft-forgotten feature of freedom – that our individual freedom is inextricably intertwined with the freedom of others, at the very least all of the citizens that make up our state or polity. More exactly, in his autobiography, Mandela says the following about freedom in South Africa:

> Freedom is indivisible; the chains on any one of my people were the chains on all of them; the chains on all of my people were the chains on me. It was during those long and lonely years [in the struggle for freedom] that my hunger for the freedom of my own people became a hunger for the freedom of all people, white and black. I knew as well as I knew anything that the oppressor must be liberated just as surely as the oppressed. A man who takes away another man's freedom is a prisoner of hatred, he is locked behind the bars of prejudice and narrow-mindedness. I am not truly free if I am taking away someone else's freedom, just as surely as I am not free when my freedom is taken from me. The oppressed and the oppressor alike are robbed of their humanity. When I walked out of prison, that was my mission, to liberate the oppressed and the oppressor both. Some say that has now been achieved. But I know that is not the case. The truth is we are not yet free; we have merely achieved the freedom to be free, the right not to be oppressed. We have not taken the final step of our journey but the first step on a longer even more difficult road. For to be free is not merely to cast off one's chains but to live in a way that respects and enhances the freedom of others.[6]

Mandela is still right. He is right that freedom depends on liberating the oppressor and the oppressed, something seen with clarity by only a handful of political thinkers before him.[7] Mandela is also still right that South Africans are not yet free, especially if freedom is power in the ways I maintain here.

More specifically, I argue that there are four main causes for the lack of freedom that prevails in South Africa: levels of poverty, inequality, unemployment and general quality of life statistics that are appalling for a middle-income country (South Africa is one of the most unequal places on earth); a public education system that fails to provide most students with basic literacy and numeracy, not to speak of readiness for tertiary education, further training or work; skewed economic and political representation and macroeconomic policy that reproduce elites rather than generate economic opportunity and political power for all; and

[6]   N. Mandela, *Long Walk to Freedom: The Autobiography of Nelson Mandela* (Johannesburg: Macdonald Purnell, 1995), pp. 616–617.
[7]   Rousseau, *Social Contract*; G. W. F. Hegel, *Phenomenology of Spirit*, ed. A. V. Miller and J. N. Findlay (Oxford: Oxford University Press, 1977 [1807]); K. Marx, *The Communist Manifesto*, ed. G. Stedman-Jones (London: Penguin, 2002 [1848]).

an electoral system that implements the idea of proportional representation so literally that it undermines rather than instantiates meaningful representation. These persistent, unresolved problems structure the book's chapters. They are the legacy of South Africa's apartheid past but also of its current lack of meaningful representation. The conjunction of these features of life in South Africa means that most South Africans find they are unable to act freely across most, if not all, of the four dimensions of freedom outlined above. The power relations within South Africa generate situations of domination that persist across all of these four dimensions; and, most importantly, the existing forms of economic and political representation reinforce these states of domination rather than act as means of rupturing them.

This claim is likely to surprise readers from right across the political spectrum because it flies in the face of an alleged obvious conclusion that a number of the evident truths about South Africa together safeguard the freedom of South Africans: South Africa's recent political liberation and the relatively long history of its liberation movement (now governing party), the ANC; its lauded, progressive, liberal constitution; its carefully 'pacted' and relatively peaceful transition to democracy; its relative economic wealth; its long-functioning institutions[8]; and the supposed fact that while a poor South African is not empowered and thus lacks freedom in many ways, the same cannot be said of wealthy South Africans. In response, I argue here that while all these (bar the last) may be true, it does not follow that South Africans are free. In doing so, I marshal two related arguments that emerge from my account of freedom as power. First, even if, say, one has freedom as power across three of the four dimensions of freedom I discuss, one's lack of power in only one is sufficient to make one lack freedom to a debilitating degree. Second, and more importantly, the lack of freedom experienced by certain groups or classes across all or any of these dimensions often has the effect of undermining the freedom of other groups or classes within the society in question. For example, as is discussed in detail in Chapter 2, although the effects of poverty and inequality on the poor are stark and obvious in that they impose a series of material and psychological obstacles to their freedom as power, the effects of high levels of poverty and inequality are similarly, if not equally, disempowering for wealthy South Africans: the levels of crime, jealousy and fear that high levels of inequality and poverty generate in any society, but particularly in South Africa, lead the

---

[8] I. Shapiro and K. Tebeau, *After Apartheid: Reinventing South Africa* (Charlottesville: University of Virginia Press, 2011), p. 8.

wealthy either to disempower themselves by shutting themselves off from the wider community behind barbed wire and high walls or become disempowered by the anxieties, phobias and illnesses these conditions generate.

Either way, while the poor South African under current conditions remains the real loser in terms of freedom as power, it is a mistake for the wealthy to think that they can secure their freedom simply by means of removing themselves physically or mentally from the society in which they live. Just as in the case of the religious retreat, who, perhaps guided by Epictetus, Jesus Christ, Gautama (later known as Buddha) or Seneca, assumes incorrectly that freedom is fully realizable only under conditions in which one has freed oneself from the necessities imposed on one by nature and politics – *from* one's body, one's desires and one's engagement with other selves – *reality bites* at some point. And when *reality bites*, the folly of thinking about freedom in either purely private or mental/spiritual terms comes home to roost, either directly, by way of crime, or indirectly, by way of a whole series of debilitating psychological and physical responses to being exposed to and by the lives and threats of the less wealthy.

In other words, I defend the idea that South Africans are not yet free for reasons slightly different from the ones suggested by Mandela, but in doing so I maintain that his general claim is a valid one. One associated caveat is important: in contrast to Mandela's emphasis on moral duty, I go on to propose that if we follow my argument regarding freedom is power through to its logical conclusion, especially in the case of South Africa, it becomes unambiguously clear to any realistic observer that it is not each South African's sense of duty to the freedom of others that will enable all South Africans to be free. Rather, it is the realization by each South African that their own individual freedom depends upon the freedom of others in their society, and that it is in each of their own individual interests to help secure the freedom (as power) of all members of their society, in particular through meaningful and efficacious economic and political representation. So, in sum, South Africans are not yet free, despite South Africa's successful transition to democracy, despite Mandela's prudent early guidance and grace, despite its lauded constitution and 20 years of consolidating democracy; and this is the case because, if freedom depends on real power for all citizens through effective political representation, so far political freedom in South Africa has not produced freedom for South Africans.

In the main body of the book I describe South Africa's current social and economic realities, but the book's main, four-fold contribution is to *explain* these conditions via a theoretical and empirical link amongst power, freedom and representation. (1) It argues that the real source of lack of freedom for the majority of the population in South Africa is brought about by the forms of economic and political representation that obtain therein. (2) This lack of freedom as regards the poorly represented majority translates into a lack of freedom for all, even the very rich, guarded (or imprisoned) behind high walls, gated communities and electric fences. (3) Some balk at the idea of associating political representation with individual freedom, but this book shows that, in South Africa, as elsewhere, properly understood, representation can generate real individual power and thus freedom. (4) In modern states like South Africa economic and political representatives are caught up in a web of judgements and decisions as the state, via political representatives, 'develops' its national economy. However, the buck stops with the political representatives; and, in the case of South Africa, they have failed dismally to free their citizens from the shackles of a violent, racist and barbaric colonial and apartheid history. Thus, besides explaining why real freedom has not followed from the attainment of political freedom, *Are South Africans Free?* also shows how rethinking the nature of freedom and representation from the perspective of South Africa helps with similar dilemmas all across the globe, as this book's second epigraph suggests.

Before I offer a synopsis of the book's chapters, I provide two short explanations for the amount of theory that remains necessary for understanding the situation in South Africa. First, *Are South Africans Free?* is not a theoretical book, but in order for the empirical case to have purchase, Chapter 1 includes a short theoretical overview of the various debates around freedom and liberty and an outline of my account of freedom as power, covered quickly in accessible, non-formal terms, requiring no specialized knowledge. Second, besides the wealth of quality-of-life statistical data now made available by various governmental, non-governmental and international agencies, all of which confirm this book's main argument, *Are South Africans Free?* focuses on the important role that representation plays in enabling or disabling freedom. The beginning of the third chapter therefore also requires a short theoretical overview of the various accounts of representation in the theoretical literature and whose combination I propose as the most felicitous, especially regarding the practical problem tackled by the book. Again these are laid out succinctly and clearly and no specialist knowledge is assumed.

Besides the introduction and conclusion, the book has four main chapters. Chapter 1, entitled 'Political Freedom?', constitutes an historical overview of how political freedom was attained in South Africa. The chapter begins with a short account of the various ways in which freedom has been understood for millennia and a defence of the idea of 'freedom as power' as a means of understanding real modern freedom, an account of freedom with a long and rich history, but one that has been ignored in recent debates on the topic of freedom or liberty; and why this alternative account of freedom provides better explanatory and normative force for arguments and demands regarding freedom and power. I then focus on the decisions that lead to the fall of apartheid, and some of the main details and events of South Africa's relatively peaceful transition to democracy, especially as regards the substance of the Freedom Charter and the various decisions made in drafting a new constitution, a new electoral system and a new structure for the various arms of government. Most importantly, in doing so I focus on why various important decisions were made regarding institutional and constitutional design and macroeconomic policy choices and how the power relations between the two main negotiating parties gave rise to an elite compromise around the idea of human rights, its principles, lexicon and associated legal and political institutions. The chapter ends by arguing that, given South Africa's recent social, economic and political history, the freedom as power of most South Africans is very far from being achieved: most South Africans are still dominated in at least one of four ways in which citizens can be dominated in terms of determining and satisfying their needs and interests and determining who should rule and how they might best rule.

In Chapter 2, 'Quality of Life', I argue that although South Africa has come a very long way since the release of Mandela and the acquisition of political freedom, as regards poverty, inequality, unemployment and education, the picture is much bleaker. This chapter uses material taken from a number of primary and secondary sources to assess South Africans' quality of life in general, and conditions of poverty, inequality, unemployment and education in particular. The most recent South African Census (2011) as compared to all of those conducted since 1994, Statistics South Africa, the October Household Surveys (OHSs), the Income and Expenditure Surveys (IESs), the (now Quarterly) Labour Force Surveys (LFSs), Poverty Net, Afrobarometer, the United Nations, the World Bank and the South African Institute of Race Relations, as well as numerous secondary sources, are all used to provide a clear portrait of conditions today as compared to both 10 years and 20 years back (at the dawn of democracy in South Africa). In all four categories, with the exception of the proportion of people living under conditions of extreme poverty, conditions have remained the same or even worsened over the last 20 years. The chapter then shows, with the help of a new wave of literature comparing quality of life across various different countries and regions, as well as local studies that corroborate this evidence, the disempowering (even enslaving) effects of poverty, inequality, unemployment and poor education on the majority of the population. Why have things not improved, despite political freedom? The chapter ends with an indication that the answer to this question is to be found in the forms of economic and political representation that democratic South Africa has embraced and how these fail to empower individual citizens to control adequately the representatives that they choose to rule them.

In Chapter 3, 'Political Representation', I argue that the answer to the conundrum of two decades of mostly failed promises regarding macroeconomic management and government responsiveness to the needs of the citizenry has its source in South Africa's macro-political forms of representation. In doing so, I suggest the South African case complicates much of the received opinion regarding the consolidation of representative democracy. I argue that the really important answer to the question regarding whether or not a democracy has been consolidated has to do with the nature of the institutions of political representation that obtain therein and the extent to which they minimize domination and thereby constrain or enable freedom as power amongst the citizenry. My focus here is on South Africa, but in order to determine whether its new representative democracy is healthy, empowering and likely to survive, in this chapter I elucidate first the notion of representation in relation to groups, classes, individuals and freedom as power. I then move on to the South African situation proper and argue that, in the light of my analysis of representation, there are *two* glaring 'gaps' and associated persistent forms of domination that the existing South African system of political representation falls short on. In the first case, it tends to close a gap that ought to be kept open; in the second case, it widens a gap it should be closing. First, South Africa's political representatives too readily succumb to the authoritarian temptation to close the gap between themselves and 'the people', or at least their representation thereof: they associate 'the party' with 'the people' and thus 'the state'. Second, South Africa's macro-political system has created *too much of a gap* between political representatives and citizens, especially as regards to how the latter are able to articulate their needs and whether and how the government responds to and evaluates these needs. As I go on to argue, the first is related to an ill-conceived response to the second, but it has also to do with the ANC's history as a liberation movement and is, undoubtedly, a consequence of the electoral system chosen by the two groups of elites involved in a self-seeking compromise during the transition to democracy.

In particular, I describe, explain and question the wisdom of full, closed party-list proportional representation, as adopted following the overthrow of apartheid in South Africa. This form of electoral system disallows meaningful citizen agency, especially as regards control and critique over powerful economic and political elites (or representatives). It hamstrings the capacity of citizens to articulate their real needs and interests and the capacity of the government to respond to these. This is the case because the institutional matrices that obtain are, as it were, predetermined to favour those groups and individuals with power in the highly unequal status quo as against those without power or access to power. In general, then, existing forms of representation in South Africa not only fail to enable citizens to overcome various forms of domination but also generate an environment that is conducive to numerous practices that are deleterious to overcoming domination and generating liberty through political representation, practices such as pervasive rent-seeking, one-party dominance, corruption and impunity amongst representatives, centralized executive power and a dangerous overemphasis on unity and solidarity. The chapter ends by explaining how South Africa could have got itself into this predicament. The answer, I argue, lies in the nature of the elite compromise determined during the transition to democracy. The moral then is that elite compromises of the kind experienced in South Africa may enable a relatively peaceful transition to democracy, but their unique focus on existing elite interests sacrifices future freedom and stability at the altar of short-term strategy and security.

Then, in Chapter 4, 'Elite Compromise', I focus on the details of the compromise, especially as it has been played out in macroeconomic policy choice in general and the management of public debt in particular. I begin with a short historical account of the two components of the compromise: political and economic. I argue that one of the main reasons that so many South Africans still lack freedom is a result of a set of macroeconomic decisions made quite soon after liberation, in which the new governing elite, an alliance led by the ANC, decided to opt for an austere set of fiscal and monetary policies and as regards borrowing for 'development'. This decision was made in the hope that 'steadying the ship of state' financially would retain local capital and state creditors and attract foreign direct investment and thus help drive growth. In other words, the new political elite thought that *not* reneging on apartheid debt would ensure against frightening away the economic representatives of existing and potential domestic and foreign investors. Moreover, as exemplified in their management of public debt since 1994, they swallowed hook, line and sinker the economic orthodoxies of the age, in order they thought to enhance their sovereign power. The tragic irony of these decisions is that not only has the exact opposite been the case – they now have less, not more, sovereign power – but it was made at the expense of righting the wrongs of the past through redistribution and the recalibration of power relations, that is, at the expense of the well-being and freedom of the majority of previously disadvantaged South Africans. The compromise was therefore made in the interests of both sets of elites – new political and old economic – and at the expense of the interests of the majority of the population. Moreover, these decisions were completely counterproductive even in their own terms: they have not secured the necessary inflows of international capital or foreign direct investment (FDI). As I argue, this has been the case for two related reasons: (a) given the inadequate response to socio-economic and political power relations that it entailed, and the fact that the old economic elite, only partially in the process of being transformed, do not have sufficient formal representation in parliament and so cannot act as a veto on policy formation, uncertainty still prevails for investors in South Africa or South African government bonds; (b) unresolved social cleavages based on extreme levels of inequality and unemployment generate violent conflicts or the constant threat of them (leading, in some instances, to brutal repression by the state, as exemplified recently by the horrors of Marikana), which further exacerbates economic uncertainty. What follows from this is that South Africa remains a risky place in which to invest, at least in the eyes of potential international investors. In other words, the political elites in democratic South Africa have failed dismally to free their citizens from the shackles imposed by a distorted, racist and barbaric colonial and apartheid history.

The concluding chapter to this book, 'Overcoming South Africans' Lack of Freedom', draws all the various threads together and provides a set of positive institutional proposals for the achievement and maintenance of freedom in South Africa. I first return to Mandela's prophetic words regarding freedom, but show more specifically why I dissent from, in particular, Mandela's emphasis on the force of our supposed *moral* duty to enhance and respect the freedom of others. As argued throughout the book, I maintain that freedom as power in South Africa does not depend on goodwill, charity or duty, or on the complete realization of those political and civil liberties currently safeguarded in its constitution, though these may help. Rather it depends on courageous leadership, active and sometimes disobedient citizenship, as yet unrealized forms of economic and political representation, and macroeconomic policy formation and implementation that leads to radical redistribution of the actual and potential wealth and opportunities offered by South Africa. I then focus on the institutional changes that would help bring this about, particularly those central to overcoming the systemic shortfalls regarding economic and political representation identified in the main body of the book. In short, I argue that South Africa will only attain and safeguard freedom if it institutionalizes the following changes: first, radical redistribution of material assets of a variety of forms; second, a completely new electoral system that mixes proportional representation and constituency-based systems; third, new forms of political representation in addition to national, periodic elections, such as, (i) a revitalized consiliar system for transferring information regarding needs and interests efficiently and impartially from the local to national level; (ii) political institutions that generate representatives who can check the decisions of existing economic and political elites, political institutions whose representatives would therefore have to be partisan vis-à-vis the interests of the 'common good' (for in South Africa, as elsewhere, the 'common good' is normally an effective cover for the interests of powerful elites), that is, partisan political institutions that would enable the expression, representation and response to the interests of the class of citizens who are currently poorly represented – the working class and the unemployed in South Africa; (iii) a decennial plebiscite enabling and controlling amendments to the substance of the constitution, particularly as it pertains to ensuring freedom as power through representation.

In sum, this book argues that poverty, inequality, rampant unemployment, poor public education, a distorted electoral system and misguided macroeconomic policy are the main reasons for the lack of freedom that still plagues South Africa, and that all of these are not reducible to but can be explained by a mistaken understanding of freedom that fails to take account of the central importance of meaningful and empowering forms of representation. Thus, in the end, although many of Mandela's sentiments regarding freedom underpin this critique of South Africa's polity and economy, this book contests Mandela's claim regarding the force of our moral duty to others to enhance their freedom. Although moral duty may play some part, this account submits that it will be a bit part. Rather, it argues that it is the self-interested realization that our individual *liberty through representation* depends upon the freedom as power of others that would motivate South African citizens to secure the freedom as power of all South Africans.

1

Political Freedom?

Similar to many other liberation struggles, the one led by the African National Congress (ANC) in South Africa made liberal use of the notion of freedom and liberty: freedom from alien rule, freedom from apartheid; the liberty to vote and stand for office; the right to love, to bring up one's children, to live securely and to trade, not determined by the colour of one's skin, one's gender or sexuality; the freedom and power to determine who represents one in the courts, the executive and the legislature; and so on. The ANC is no liberationist upstart. There have been moments when its very survival was in question, but its history has been long and synonymous with the struggle for political freedom and the advent of democracy in South Africa. On 8 January 2012 it celebrated its centenary, only a little over 2 years prior to the celebration of two decades of democracy in South Africa. Most importantly, if not always completely worked out, its focus on freedom from alien rule, colonialism and apartheid consistently involved a sense of what might be necessary for the real, concrete, everyday freedom of all South Africans within a democratic South Africa. This is evident in nearly every strategy and policy document or publication ever since its founding in 1912, and in particular: the 1943 *Africans' Claims* in South Africa document; the 1955 Freedom Charter; the causes and consequences of the 1960 Sharpeville and 1976 Soweto apartheid massacres; the 1989 Harare Declaration; and from even before 1989 right up until 1996, during the negotiations with the National Party (NP) prior to and in the early years of rule in a democratic South Africa; and, as a party in government, in some of its early macroeconomic policy choices, for example, the Reconstruction and Development Programme (RDP). Moreover, the nature and maintenance of freedom are still very much at the forefront of debate in democratic South Africa, due in no small part to the nature of South Africa's constitution and recent real threats on specific freedoms, such as the constraints on freedom of expression that will follow if Zuma signs in to law The Protection of State Information Bill (popularly known as The Secrecy Bill).

This is not a book about the history of the ANC, so I will not chart its long, adaptive and fascinating history, the best examples of which can be found in the scholarly works of William Beinart, Anthony Butler, Saul Dubow and Tom Lodge, amongst others.[1] Few other liberation movements, at least in Africa, can claim such a long and illustrious history. Nor can many claim such versatility, adaptability and courage in the face of 300 years of colonial 'white' supremacy and segregation culminating in nearly half a century of institutionalized apartheid and racial domination. The movement's history is marked by a fluid capacity to change, to grasp new opportunities and to seize the moment at various important junctures in South Africa's history. What began as a gathering of rebellious chiefs and mission-educated elites, who led it during its early years, later supplemented by urban workers, rural activists, organized women, the youth, communist allies and middle-class leaders, is now South Africa's ruling party with high levels of organization and skills. However, the great promise of the ANC's Freedom Charter, the internationalization of its fight for freedom, the eventual overthrow of apartheid and the relatively peaceful transition to democratic rule in South Africa have given way to very little real political and economic change for the lives of most South Africans. As is analysed in detail in the next chapter, South Africa remains one of the most unequal places on earth, with some of the highest unemployment rates in the world and dangerously high youth unemployment (above 50%), alongside crippling numbers of often violent strikes. The price of its peaceful transition to democratic rule and the ANC's desire to attract international investment has been macroeconomic policy that hinders rather than helps the new South African polity in its attempts to respond to the dire need to overcome the legacies of apartheid. Formal political freedom might have been obtained, but this has not been followed by real political freedom. What went wrong?

In this chapter I begin to answer this question by, first, defending an argument for what I call 'freedom is power', which serves two functions: as I argue in the concluding chapter, it may yet help to reset South Africa's political and economic compass towards concrete, real political freedom; and, more importantly for my purposes in this chapter, it enables a more lucid lens through which to understand what has gone wrong in the objective to free South Africans. Using this new theoretical template regarding freedom I then go on to argue that, in particular, three important moments in the ANC's history indicate and explain the extent

---

[1] W. Beinart, *Twentieth-Century South Africa* (Oxford: Oxford University Press, 2001); A. Butler, *The Idea of the ANC* (Johannesburg: Jacana, 2012); S. Dubow, *The African National Congress* (Johannesburg: Jonathan Ball, 2000) and T. Lodge, *Sharpeville: An Apartheid Massacre and Its Consequences* (Oxford: Oxford University Press, 2011).

to which it was willing to accept and even reinforce the international political language and institutions of human rights, which, once RDP had been shelved, accommodated very comfortably the associated macroeconomic choices that set South Africa on a strictly orthodox and conservative path of development through growth as opposed to development through industrialization: the adoption of fiscal and monetarist orthodoxy rather than the realignment of the South African economy for effective redistribution of wealth and opportunities and the creation of political institutions that would enable real political freedom. These moments are the Freedom Charter, the Sharpeville and Soweto massacres, and the negotiations with the NP and the early years of rule in democratic South Africa that produced a constitution based on human rights and forms of economic policy and political representation that have hamstrung any attempts to attain freedom as power for all South Africans. The main claim I defend, in the face of most mainstream interpretations, is that the language of real political freedom for all, if understood in terms of human rights, which finds its full, final expression in the constitution of 1996, was never in contradiction with an austere, conservative approach to fiscal and monetary policy, a subsequent increase in corruption, patronage politics, and various forms of malfeasance and the empowerment of a small economic and political elite, which may have partly changed its 'colour' but has done little or nothing to change the basic power relations that were inherited from apartheid. The very internationalization of the anti-apartheid movement and the associated uncritical or even instrumental adoption of the United Nations-inspired language of human rights[2] is ironically and tragically, especially given recent events in Marikana, one of the main reasons for the lack of freedom as power that currently afflicts the lives of all South Africans. In other words, in South Africa it is not so much a case of 'revolution suspended'[3] as 'revolution still pending' or the 'revolution is still to be televised', to paraphrase the 1960s' protest movements in the United States of America and, later, Gil Scott-Heron's famous song.

Freedom as power

Freedom is power, as defended here, is an amalgam of components of the various liberation struggles that have peppered our shared histories and a response to the practical inadequacies of the three main received theoretical accounts of freedom

[2] Dubow, *African National Congress.*
[3] A. Habib, *South Africa's Suspended Revolution: Hopes and Prospects* (Johannesburg: Wits University Press, 2013).

that have characterized human history: Republican freedom, 'negative' freedom and 'positive' freedom (aspects of the latter two combine in practice, in manifold ways, to produce 'Liberal' freedom). Freedom is power is quite distinct from both these 'Liberal' and Republican mainstreams in two important senses. First, it does not abstract liberty from two related concepts – power and representation – that would otherwise ground freedom in the substantive individual and political capacities for real emancipation. Second, it therefore does not *reduce* freedom to one of the following three defining features: (1) the absence of (external) impediments; (2) the ability to decide for oneself what to do (self-determination); or (3) citizenship within a free state. These are, originally, Jeremy Bentham's, but more famously, Isaiah Berlin's 'negative' and 'positive' conceptions of freedom and the rival Republican account, respectively.[4] Understood in all of these terms, South Africans are now free, despite the evident lack of real power to act freely that characterizes the lives of most – particularly the unemployed and working class – who live in this highly unequal, impoverished, racially scarred and unsafe society. These theories or conceptions of freedom are therefore unpersuasive, especially given the fact that they are proposed as universally applicable theories. So, to see clearly *why* South Africans lack freedom we need to start elsewhere, with an account of freedom understood in terms of the power to act and the requirements for that power. In other words, in capturing the concrete nature of freedom by linking freedom to real and effective power, this alternative account rejects the common tendency to favour a minimalist account of freedom over a realistic one.

There is nothing crazy about this idea, even though it may elicit strong countervailing responses. When I say 'I am free' normally I am not saying exclusively 'I live in a free state' or 'I am externally unimpeded' or 'I am self-determining'. No, what I usually mean is 'I am free to do X', which concretely

---

[4] J. Bentham, *Of Laws in General*, ed. H.L.A. Hart (Oxford: Oxford University Press, 1970 [ca. 1782]); I. Berlin, 'Two Concepts of Liberty', in *Four Essays on Liberty* (Oxford: Oxford University Press, 1996 [1969]), pp. 118–172; C. Taylor, 'What's Wrong With Negative Liberty', in *The Idea of Freedom*, ed. A. Ryan (Oxford: Oxford University Press, 1979), pp. 175–193; N. Machiavelli, *The Discourses*, ed. B. Crick, trans. by L. J. Walker with revisions by B. Richardson (London: Penguin, 2003 [ca. 1517]); J.-J. Rousseau, *The Social Contract*, in J.-J. Rousseau, *The Social Contract and Other Later Political Writings*, ed. V. Gourevitch (Cambridge: Cambridge University Press, 1997 [1762]); Q. Skinner, 'The Idea of Negative Liberty', in *Philosophy in History*, ed. R. Rorty, J. B. Schneewind and Q. Skinner (Cambridge: Cambridge University Press, 1984), pp. 193–224; Q. Skinner, 'Machiavelli's *Discorsi* and the Pre-humanist Origins of Republican Ideas', in *Machiavelli and Republicanism*, ed. G. Bock, Q. Skinner and M. Viroli (Cambridge: Cambridge University Press, 1991), pp. 121–142; Q. Skinner, *Liberty Before Liberalism* (Cambridge: Cambridge University Press, 1998); Q. Skinner, 'The Idea of Negative Liberty: Machiavellian and Modern Perspectives', in *Vision of Politics Vol II Renaissance Virtues* (Cambridge: Cambridge University Press, 2002), pp. 186–212; Q. Skinner, *Hobbes and Republican Liberty* (Cambridge: Cambridge University Press, 2008); P. Pettit, *Republicanism: A Theory of Freedom and Government* (Oxford: Clarendon Press, 1997); P. Pettit, *On The People's Terms* (Cambridge: Cambridge University Press, 2012).

means 'I have the power or ability to do *X*'. Hence, real modern freedom here is identified with and *as* power in that it conceives of freedom as a *combination of my ability to determine what I will do and my power to do it or bring it about*.

Nor is this a particularly novel idea. Freedom as power in this sense chimes well with most of the struggles for freedom across the ages, including the sharp distinction between freedom and slavery in Antiquity and beyond, subsequent slave revolts like the Haitian Revolution and later liberation struggles against colonialism, apartheid and domination, *and* the everyday attempts to gain more independence and freedom from, say, the state, the churches, the community, the law, poverty, crime and so on. As Frantz Fanon argues, the human condition is to be free and that freedom resides in the *capacity* to choose and to act.[5]

It turns out, moreover, that thinking about freedom as both about being able to *determine* what one will do and having the *power* to do what one decides to do is more common in the western tradition than is normally supposed. Despite much received opinion, a surprising number and variety of political thinkers from right across the political spectrum associate freedom and power in exactly these terms. It is a mainstay of much of antiquity. As the Roman historian Titus Livy put it, 'freedom is to be in one's own power', by which he meant *not* the autonomy of the will, but self-reliance, enjoyed of right by Roman citizens, the conditions for which were secured by law and within social relations of respect and reciprocity.[6] This is also true of a number of modern thinkers, as diverse as Thomas Hobbes, the progenitor of the idea of 'negative' freedom, the idea of freedom as absence of external impediments, Jean-Jacques Rousseau, a central figure in the opposing, Republican canon, Edmund Burke and John Stuart Mill.[7] Thus, a whole array of thinkers, even thinkers that Berlin lauds as standard-bearers for his 'negative' conception of freedom, are ultimately concerned with whether or not someone is able to exercise his or her power to act, that is, to bring something about, to do something.

However, it is in the work of Karl Marx that we find the full efflorescence of the account of freedom that underpins my argument here. In *The German Ideology*, and in other later works, Marx distinguishes three concepts of liberty. The first is

---

[5] F. Fanon, *Black Skin, White Masks*, trans. C. L. Markmann (London: Pluto Press, 1986), p. 160.

[6] T. Livy, *History of Rome from Its Foundation: Rome and the Mediterranean [Ab Urbe Condita]*, trans. H. Bettenson (London: Penguin, 2005) 35.32.11; Ch. Wirszubski, *Libertas as a Political Idea at Rome during the Late Republic and Early Principate* (Cambridge: Cambridge University Press, 1968), pp. 8–9; and below.

[7] T. Hobbes, *Leviathan*, ed. R. Tuck (Cambridge: Cambridge University Press, 1996 [1651]), pp. 91, 146; Rousseau, *The Social Contract*, p. 82; E. Burke, *Reflections on the Revolution in France*, ed. and intro. Conor Cruise O'Brien (London: Penguin, 2004 [1790]), p. 91; J.S. Mill, *On Liberty and Other Essays*, ed. John Gray (Oxford: Oxford University Press, 2008 [1859]), pp. 7, 16–17, 116, 121–122.

what Marx associates with the anarchism of Max Stirner, but in today's parlance
we would call 'negative' freedom or, more exactly, the 'pure negative' freedom
of libertarianism.[8] The second concept of freedom Marx discusses he identifies
with Immanuel Kant's view of freedom and which he defines as the ability a
creature has to make its own decisions, or govern itself.[9] Kant is quite explicit
that, for him, freedom is the mere ability to determine the will, irrespective
of whether this is even translated into actual action in the world. The third
concept of freedom is the one Marx calls the 'materialist' notion of freedom
that identifies freedom with power and that he thinks is the full, sophisticated
notion. Following this account, freedom comprises 'the conjunction of the
ability to determine what one will do and the power to do what one decides to
do', and anything less than this is a mere shadow of the concept of freedom.[10]
This means that for Marx the other two concepts he discusses, and *a fortiori* the
main three concepts analysed in the modern literature, are poor approximations
of this real form of freedom.

Freedom as power also captures the fact that people are interested in
freedom as a human ideal, goal or aspiration because it is connected with the
actual attainment of 'something', that is, some good or set of goods; and the
actual attainment of these depends on my having the *power* to attain them.
The liberation struggle in South Africa, for example, did not have as its goal
the abstract idea of being 'free from impediment' or 'living in a free state'.
Rather, it had more concrete political, economic and social goals: being free to
determine who rules and how they rule, to produce, exchange and consume
wherever and whenever, to love, procreate, entertain oneself and others, bring
up one's children and so on; and to do so in conditions free of poverty and racial
and gender discrimination and domination. This is strongly in evidence in the
ANC's Freedom Charter, in demands such as

> [e]very man and woman shall have the right to vote for and to stand as a
> candidate for all bodies which make laws; ... [a]ll people shall have equal
> rights to trade where they choose, to manufacture and enter all trades, crafts
> and professions; ... [t]he law shall guarantee to all their right to speak, to
> organize, to meet together, to publish, to preach, to worship and to educate their

---

[8] K. Marx and F. Engels, *The German Ideology*, in *Marx Engels Collected Works*, Volume 5 (London:
    Lawrence and Wishart, 1976 [ca. 1846]), pp. 304–306; I. Carter, *A Measure of Freedom* (Oxford:
    Oxford University Press, 1999); M. H. Kramer, *The Quality of Freedom* (Oxford: Oxford University
    Press, 2003); H. Steiner, 'Individual Liberty', in *The Liberty Reader*, ed. D. Miller (Edinburgh:
    Edinburgh University Press, 2006), pp. 123–140; R. Geuss, 'On the Very Idea of a Metaphysics of
    Right', in *Politics and the Imagination* (Princeton: Princeton University Press, 2010), pp. 56–57.
[9] Marx and Engels, *The German Ideology*, pp. 193–195.
[10] Ibid., pp. 305–306; Geuss, 'On the Very Idea of a Metaphysics of Right', p. 57.

children; ... [a]ll people shall have the right to live where they please, be decently housed, and to bring up their families in comfort and security ... [t]he courts shall be representative of all the people ... [and] the rights of the people shall be the same regardless of race, colour or sex.[11]

As it is in the Constitution of the Republic of South Africa, 1996, by means of its repeated reference to the injustices of the apartheid past, the representative institutions of the new South Africa, and a comprehensive bill of rights that secures not only civil and political rights but also social and economic rights, such as 'freedom of trade, occupation and profession', 'human dignity', 'environment', 'housing', 'health care', 'education', and so on and so forth.[12]

In other words, as both of these founding documents for a free and democratic South Africa make clear, the attainment of political liberation is only one step towards securing and maintaining freedom as power – both display acute awareness that political freedom is an ongoing process of enabling the power of the citizenry. To paraphrase Mandela in the first epigraph to this book, the attainment of political liberation alone does not secure real political freedom. Fanon too makes a very similar claim in relation to post-colonies in general and with particular reference to the importance of how freedom is only manifest in concrete terms, such as in access to 'land', 'bread' and the other requirements necessary for 'human dignity'.[13] In other words, political liberation from alien rule is a necessary but not sufficient condition for the broader concrete goals and conditions for freedom as power. (And, as I discuss below, the attainment of these broader goals depends on the active generation, defence and exercise of various other powers within a free state.)

The same is true for less-stark struggles for freedom under less-tyrannical conditions. The constant clamour for freedom of speech or freedom of academic enterprise, to take but two examples, is normally associated with a whole set of perceived goods. Citizens, the press, academics and artists normally do not defend press, academic and artistic freedom – that, for example, the press should be free to print what they see fit and that university lecturers should be free to teach and research as they see fit – simply because they dislike being constrained or because they think freedom depends upon being able to act unimpeded. They do so because they think this form of freedom brings with it a whole series of associated benefits that we ought to safeguard and value, such as, the power to

---

[11] ANC, 2011. The Freedom Charter [online]. Available from: http://www.anc.org.za/show.php?id=72 [Accessed 30 July, 2013].

[12] *Constitution of the Republic of South Africa*, Eighth Edition (Cape Town: Juta & Co Ltd, 2009).

[13] F. Fanon, *The Wretched of the Earth* (Paris: Présence Africaine, 1963) p. 43.

criticise our governments, the power to hold them accountable, the associated requisite power to disseminate information, generate new findings and ideas, and so on. This has been much in evidence both in the recent controversies around attempts by the ANC government to legislate what is potentially, at least in its first few incarnations, a draconian Secrecy Bill, to censor art that criticises those in political power *and* in various responses by academics in South Africa to withstand government intervention into university curricula and debates regarding the manner in which they do, or ought to, carry out their research. Many, of course, undoubtedly simply recoil and spit back at the attempted interference, but the more subtle, nuanced and intelligent responses display a keen awareness of the way in which these long-fought-for freedoms are necessary for a set of political, economic and scientific goods: the power of citizens to keep political and economic elites accountable; the power to determine and disseminate information regarding the country's economic and political elites; and the importance for scientific endeavour itself and the social, economic and political health of one's society that the practice of academic research and teaching and artistic expression be enabled by certain fundamental freedoms.

Moreover, in all three cases – the case of liberation from apartheid, claims for freedom of speech and demands for artistic and academic freedom – the attainment of these goals or benefits, these various freedoms, depends upon those involved having the *power* to attain them. It is an often forgotten fact of history that the freedoms associated with political liberation from apartheid South Africa, for example, were only attainable when the various components of the struggle against apartheid gained the power (or at least perceived power) to overcome the apartheid state. That it was a successful and relatively peaceful transition was due to the coming together of a whole series of powers and events – an *impasse* between the military power of the NP and the popular power of the ANC, strong international pressure, an internal front of opposition led by the United Democratic Front (UDF), an economy in freefall, the courage of a few leaders within both the ANC and the NP leadership and so on – none of which were inevitable or whose coming to a head together was part of a broader teleology of history in the region and elsewhere. It depended upon the powers of groups and individuals who had the foresight, determination and courage to seize a historically unusual if very unpredictable moment.

Thus, another way of construing the importance of this more substantive account of freedom as power is that it enables thinking about how freedom relates to the exercise of our powers as individuals and how we are enabled and disabled by a variety of internal and external abilities, obstacles, mechanisms and power relations. This is something, again, that a number of other social and political theorists and philosophers have identified and stressed from a wide range of political perspectives. These examples not only provide further instances of the identification of freedom and power, but also emphasize the fact that freedom is about 'effective power', that is, that freedom is such an important social and political ideal and goal because it is rightly identified as a precondition for certain desirable 'beings and doings'.[14] For example, as John Dewey puts it: 'Liberty is power, effective power to do specific things... The demand of liberty is the demand for power'.[15] Surprisingly, this association is also evident at the heart of contemporary analytical political philosophy, for example, in Feinberg's account of freedom: 'There are at least two basics ideas in the conceptual complex we call "freedom"; namely, rightful self-government (autonomy), and the overall ability to do, choose or achieve things, which can be called "optionality"...'.[16]

Considered through the lenses of these and other authors and struggles for full political freedom, the main liberal argument that to be free is to act in the absence of impediments or obstacles, in particular those that result from conscious deliberate human action, rests on a deep misapprehension about politics.[17] I cannot adequately summarize here a complex argument that I develop and defend elsewhere,[18] suffice to say that liberal thinkers such as these are concerned with external obstacles because they think it is better to have *more* possible courses of action rather than fewer. This is obviously true of some situations, but it is not clear that it is true of all; but whether or not it is always a good thing to have more rather than less options open, the number of available options depends not merely on the presence or absence of obstacles, but on the conjunction of one's power and the internal or external obstacles that stand in one's way. Moreover, whether or not a person, act or institution constitutes an obstacle will itself often depend on my relative power, in particular my position within existing power relations and *vis-à-vis* existing forms of representation. I therefore argue that

---

[14] F. Nietzsche, 'Notebook 34, April–June 1885' 34[250] and 'Notebook I, Autumn 1885–Spring 1886' I[33], in *Writings from the Late Notebooks*, ed. Rüdiger Bittner (Cambridge: Cambridge University Press, 2003), pp. 16, 57.

[15] J. Dewey, *Problems of Men* (New York: Greenwood Press, 1968 [1946]), p. 111.

[16] J. Feinberg, 'Freedom and Liberty', in *Routledge Encyclopedia of Philosophy*, ed. E. Craig (London: Routledge, 1998), p. 1. Available from: http://www.rep.routledge.com/article/S026 [Accessed 4 November, 2009].

[17] J. Locke, *Two Treatises on Government* (Cambridge: Cambridge University Press, 1988 [1689]); Bentham, *Of Laws in General*; Mill, *On Liberty and Other Essays*; F. A. Hayek, *The Constitution of Liberty* (London: Routledge, 1960); Berlin, 'Two Concepts of Liberty'; Carter, *A Measure of Freedom*; Kramer, *The Quality of Freedom*; Steiner, 'Individual Liberty'.

[18] L. Hamilton, *Freedom is Power: Liberty Through Political Representation* (Cambridge: Cambridge University Press, 2014).

freedom is power in the sense that it depends upon my power, control and self-control within the four following dimensions: (a) the power to act or be as I would choose in the absence of either internal or external obstacles or both; (b) the power to determine the government of my political association or community; (c) the ability to develop and exercise my powers and capacities self-reflectively within and against existing norms, expectations and power relations; and (d) the power to determine my social and economic environment via meaningful control over my and my groups' economic and political representatives.

These are objective conditions for freedom because they are shared and because all need them as necessary conditions for the possibility of freedom of action, particularly in the sense of political agency widely construed: freedom to vote, participate, deliberate, petition, veto, impeach, determine who rules and in whose interests they rule and control these representatives, both economic and political. And these objective conditions are all political because they cannot be achieved and maintained by individual or spontaneous collective action alone: given that they depend upon social, economic and political empowerment, sacrifices, discipline and control amongst all citizens, they require the coercive force of a political authority to ensure that they are institutionalized and sustained. However objective, though, this is not an exhaustive account of individual freedom. The full extent of my claim is that whatever freedom for any particular individual may involve, under the precarious and inter-dependent nature of modern conditions it will depend on the power and control individuals are able to exercise within the four domains of freedom outlined above. The concern is therefore with the basic necessary requirements for freedom as power, or in other words, individual power and control within these four dimensions are necessary (but not sufficient) conditions for political freedom.

Freedom and representation

The problem with many political theoretical accounts of freedom is that they take the unit of agency to be either the individual or the state, that is, a single agent or a single entity with clear agency, and they build their accounts of *political* freedom upon this basis. It is no surprise then that they infrequently incorporate analyses of power relations and economic and political representation into their accounts and that they all conceive of unfreedom as necessarily having its basis in conscious deliberate human action, that is, that we are only made unfree by the conscious deliberate acts of individuals or similar agents, such as corporations or states. This is as true of the liberals and libertarians cited above as it is of modern Republican thought.[19] This is an unconvincing way of conceiving of social and political existence under most conditions of human existence, but it is particularly implausible under modern conditions, given the complexity and division of labour of life within and between modern states, characterized as it is by membership of a whole array of overlapping and interdependent groups and various forms of associated representation. Our freedom is therefore determined to a significant degree by a number of different variables to do with the nature and power of these groups and their representatives. Individual, modern freedom as power will normally not be a simple matter of direct individual control over the domains listed above but will be a matter of individual power and control, coupled with the power and control of the groups and representatives that frame and format the lives of modern individuals, complicated even further by the power relations that exist between individuals and groups and amongst the various groups themselves.

I discuss groups and group representation again in Chapters 3 and 4 when I provide the two main components for what I submit goes some way towards a complete diagnosis for why South Africa still lacks freedom. However, before proceeding with this part of the argument here, it is important to state unambiguously that the notion of 'group' as articulated here does not, for a moment, assume that any single individual's identity is determined by a group identity. Individuals can and normally are 'members' of various groups within society determined by various classes, interests, perspectives and roles.[20] Individual or group identity is therefore not conceived of as essential and unchanging. Rather, resorting to the language of 'groups' is shorthand for speaking about the various groups, classes and social perspectives that exist in all modern polities. Nor does anything follow from this discussion regarding group rights: along with liberals and in opposition to communitarians, if rights turn out to be the best means of formatting politics,[21] I remain sceptical of the idea of group rights, especially as regards normative or ethical primacy. Individual rights must trump group rights because group rights can and often

---

[19] E.g. Pettit, *Republicanism: A Theory of Freedom and Government* and *On the People's Terms*; but cf. Machiavelli, *The Discourses*; W. Weymans, 'Freedom Through Political Representation: Lefort, Gauchet and Rosanvallon on the Relationship Between State and Society', *European Journal of Political Theory*, 4.3 (2005), pp. 263–82; J. P. McCormick, *Machiavellian Democracy* (Cambridge: Cambridge University Press, 2011).

[20] I. Shapiro and W. Kymlicka (eds), *Ethnicity and Group Rights: NOMOS XXXIX* (New York: New York University Press, 1997); I. Marion Young, *Inclusion and Democracy* (Oxford: Oxford University Press, 2000).

[21] Something contested in Geuss, 'On the Very Idea of a Metaphysics of Right'; L. Hamilton, *The Political Philosophy of Needs* (Cambridge: Cambridge University Press, 2003) and R. Geuss and L. Hamilton 'Human Rights: A Very Bad Idea', *Theoria*, 135 (2013), pp. 83–103.

are used to justify institutions and practices that act against the empowerment of individuals. This is important particularly in the case of South Africa, given how the concept of 'group right' has been deployed historically in South Africa. Finally, however important for political understanding, the concept of 'class' is less capacious as compared to 'group', since it cannot include other kinds of group membership and associated interests, particularly those related to gender, geography, street, satisfaction and so on.

Freedom and domination

Moreover, my alternative account remains realistic about freedom and domination. Following Michel Foucault, Steven Lukes and Raymond Geuss it holds that 'power' is a relation that is connected to the abilities of agents to bring about significant affects, either by furthering their own interests or affecting the interests of others, positively or negatively.[22] These abilities depend upon the extent to which individuals are able to determine and satisfy their vital and agency needs.[23] This in turn depends on the prevailing political and economic institutions and whether or not citizens find themselves in situations of domination, or what Foucault calls 'states of domination'. Moving beyond, yet in the spirit of, Foucault, I argue that a situation or state of domination can take various forms, but in general they are characterized by power relations that block or fail to empower individuals in their attempts to determine and satisfy their needs.[24] This can take various forms. Existing power relations can: (a) mislead me in my attempts to *identify* my needs, for example, patriarchal institutions and norms; (b) ensure that I do not have the means or voice to *express* my needs, for example, apartheid South Africa; (c) disable meaningful *evaluation* of needs, for example, unregulated liberal capitalism; and (d) constrain the capacity to *meet* needs, for example, the corrupt and distorted patronage politics of post-apartheid South Africa. Freedom as power therefore depends upon avoiding or

---

[22] M. Foucault, *Power/Knowledge: Selected Interviews and Other Writings, 1972–77* (Brighton: Harvester, 1980); M. Foucault, *Discipline and Punish* (New York: Penguin, 1991 [1975]); M. Foucault, "'Omnes et Singulatim": Toward a Critique of Political Reason', in M. Foucault, *Essential Works, Vol 3: Power*, ed. J. D. Faubion (London: Penguin, 1997), pp. 298–325; M. Foucault, *The Will to Knowledge: The History of Sexuality, Vol 1*, trans. R. Hurley (London: Penguin, 1998 [1976]); S. Lukes, *Power: A Radical View*, Second Edition (New York: Palgrave Macmillan, 2005), pp. 63, 65, 109; R. Geuss, *Philosophy and Real Politics* (Princeton: Princeton University Press, 2008), p. 27.

[23] Hamilton, *Needs*.

[24] Cf. Pettit, *Republicanism: A Theory of Freedom and Government and On the People's Terms*; F. Lovett, *A General Theory of Domination and Justice* (Cambridge: Cambridge University Press, 2010).

overcoming situations of domination by ensuring control over the dimensions listed earlier via control over one's groups' representatives in general and one's political representatives in particular.

In short, individual freedom as power across the four social and political dimensions I list are the objective conditions necessary for avoiding or overcoming situations or states of domination. Moreover, given the economic and political reality within large, complex modern capitalist states, our individual freedom as power will normally not be a simple matter of direct individual control over these domains of freedom or the individual capacity to avoid these forms of domination. Modern political freedom (and avoidance of domination) is therefore determined to a significant degree by three associated matrices of freedom as power: (a) the material conditions and power of the groups that we find ourselves (or in some cases choose) to be members of; (b) the relative power of our groups' representatives; and (c) the relationship between our groups' representatives and our formal political representatives. By conceiving of freedom in terms of power and group representation, my alternative account of freedom avoids the mistakes of 'negative', 'positive' and 'republican' accounts of freedom, especially regarding the common tendency to focus uniquely on conscious deliberate human action and, at least in its libertarian form, the associated aggregation of individual freedoms to determine degrees of individual and group freedom, informed as they all are by assumptions regarding a direct relation of stylized individual autonomous agency and the freedom of the group or community.[25] And, more importantly for my argument here, it does not avoid the important link between the causal power of individuals, groups and representatives and their freedom. Or, put more positively, it provides an analytical framework for assessing the social and political power of agents as citizens and subjects, that is, as regards their actual capacities to affect and critique public policy (indirectly, via their representatives, or by means of more direct forms of participation or protest) and their abilities to determine their own and their groups' futures and act upon these determinations. This is a more realistic and comprehensive account of political freedom than existing competitor theories as it does not reduce the domain of freedom to 'private' freedom or 'freedom from politics' in some putative 'private sphere' where individuals are free from politics and the law, but nor does it flip right the other way and assume, as in Hannah Arendt's political thought, that political freedom

---

[25] E.g. Carter, *A Measure of Freedom*; Pettit, *Republicanism: A Theory of Freedom and Government* and *On the People's Terms*.

is always fully 'public and active'.[26] It remains realistic about the impossibility
of constantly active political participation under modern conditions and yet
provides means of conceiving of even the most supposedly atomistic and private
of causal powers as linked to the capacities and powers of others in one's society.
This is what I take Mandela to mean when he claims, in the long quote in the
main introduction to this book, that '[f]reedom is indivisible' – the freedom of
one depends on the freedom of all.

South Africans' lack of political freedom

As I argue in the next chapter, freedom's indivisibility is brought out well in
the South African situation, particularly if freedom is understood in terms
of power. I need first though to outline exactly why South Africans still lack
freedom as power. Surprisingly for some, maybe, this realistic account of
freedom as power sets more stringent normative and institutional standards
than other existing barometers of freedom such as the annual Freedom House
measurement, amongst others.[27] Some may see this as an advantage; some
may not. Either way, given that freedom as power admits of degree and is not
merely a matter of counting up or quantifying individual freedoms, as is the
case with these other forms of measurement and is unambiguously the case for
the libertarian conception of freedom that underpins them – '[t]he freedom of
the group is nothing other than the sum total of the degrees of freedom of its
individual members'[28] – it enables the categorization of economies and polities
in terms of their degree of freedom as power. Contemporary South Africa does
not meet these criteria even closely, despite its peaceful transition to liberal
democratic rule and lauded, liberal constitution. This is because it has failed
to eradicate or even reduce domination across all of the four domains of
freedom articulated here. It is no exaggeration to argue that under current
conditions most South Africans are still: (a) misled in their attempts to *identify*
their needs; (b) kept from having the means or voice to *express* their needs;

---

[26] H. Arendt, 'Freedom and Politics' in *The Liberty Reader*, ed. D. Miller (Edinburgh: Edinburgh
University Press, 2006 [1960]), pp. 58–79; Hamilton, *Freedom is Power*, ch. 2.

[27] Freedom House, 1973–2013, *Freedom in the World* (Washington, DC: Freedom House) Available
from: http://www.freedomhouse.org/report-types/freedom-world; R. Mattes, 'Democracy Without
People: Political Institutions and Citizenship in the New South Africa', Afrobarometer Working
Paper No. 82. Cape Town: *Institute for Democracy in South Africa (IDASA)* (November 2007) p. 10.

[28] Carter, *A Measure of Freedom*, p. 267.

(c) are unable meaningfully to *evaluate* their needs; and (d) are constrained to a debilitating degree in their capacity to *meet* their needs.

This is the case because the majority of South Africans are not empowered by the economic and political institutions and forms of representation that were adopted during and following the end of apartheid. The reason for this has to do with the nature of the settlement that was eventually reached between the two major players in the negotiated transition to democratic rule – the NP and the ANC. Informal negotiations began from the late 1980s, some time before Mandela was freed in 1990, reaching fever pitch right up until the eleventh hour prior to the 1994 elections, and finally finding entrenchment in the constitution of 1996.[29] The first thing to note is that even some time prior to President de Klerk's speech to parliament on 2 February 1990, in which he announced the unbanning of the ANC and all other previously banned parties, that all prisoners, including Mandela, were to be released and that all exiles were to be allowed to return home, there was a recognition by some in the leadership of both the NP and ANC that an *impasse* had been reached: 'a grudging recognition in each party that their adversaries had the capacity to frustrate their goals and objectives as well as being unable to achieve their own' (Turok, 2008: 41)[30]. Just as the ANC's leaders recognized that it had no hope of bringing down the apartheid regime militarily, the majority that it represented could not be kept down by military force alone; hence, the NP realized that its military might was insufficient to maintain the order and oppression necessary to return the apartheid regime and economy to its supposed heyday of the 1970s, even if it were sufficient to continue to make a mockery of the ANC as a liberation army.

This *impasse* of power between the two major parties in what was a delicate, dangerous and protracted negotiated settlement meant that both parties were forced to compromise on fundamental issues. The ANC, for example, gave way on the issue of federalism, or at least to a certain degree, ultimately played out through the formation of large urban municipalities with executive mayors,[31] and agreed to the inclusion of a right to private property and a variety of social and cultural rights within a fulsome bill of rights. The latter two compromises had been vehemently opposed by the ANC for most of the preceding half century,

---

[29] Beinart, *Twentieth-Century South Africa*; R. Spitz and M. Chaskalson, *The Politics of Transition: A Hidden History of South Africa's Negotiated Settlement* (Johannesburg: Witwatersrand University Press, 2000); H. Klug, *Constituting Democracy: Law, Globalism and South Africa's Political Reconstruction* (Cambridge: Cambridge University Press, 2000).

[30] B. Turok, *From the Freedom Charter to Polokwane: The Evolution of ANC Economic Policy* (Cape Town: New Agenda, 2008).

[31] Mattes, 'Democracy Without People'.

from the Freedom Charter of 1955 to the Harare Declaration of 1989. Both of these compromises were aimed at appeasing the realistic fear the NP had that the minority interests of those they represented under a democratic dispensation would be trampled by the majority. The NP, on the other hand, dropped its demands for a form of consociational democracy that would have, in effect, given certain minority groups veto powers over legislation, that is, it would have disproportionately empowered small, cultural groups (particularly their 'white' constituency) and protected existing privileges to a much greater degree than would be the case under any possibly conceivable form of majoritarian or popular rule.

However, it was not the compromises that were the most important effects of the *impasse*. The most telling consequence of the *impasse* was that there were a number of structural issues that both sides could agree on, partly because of the nature of the *impasse* itself – it meant that each party's erstwhile enemy was simply going to have to become a 'partner' of sorts during and following the transition to democratic rule – but also because the globally accepted and powerful human rights discourse, coincidentally, conformed with the concerns and interests of both parties. The result was a 'pacted' settlement,[32] brokered by means of an elite compromise that has effectively reinforced the lack of freedom as power of the majority of South Africans, as completely elaborated on in Chapter 4. Given the proximate history and the nature of the *impasse*, it was in neither party's interest to completely pull out of the process, to try and go it alone and get what they wanted alone; neither could, so neither did.

This was exemplified in mid-1992 when the first efforts to reach a negotiated settlement – the now famous Convention for a Democratic South Africa that convened on 20 December 1991 (dubbed CODESA one) – ground to a halt over a number of contentious issues, in particular, which body would be empowered to draft South Africa's new constitution. Both sides were able to make concessions and overcome the stalemate on the basis of the guarantees offered by the human rights discourse. The ANC accepted the idea of 'sunset clause', put forward by Communist Party Chairman Joe Slovo, providing executive power-sharing with the NP government for a period of 5 years after the democratic elections. This enabled the NP government to accept a democratic constitution-making process, rather than by negotiation in CODESA, that is, that the constitution would be drafted by an elected constituent assembly, which itself made it possible for

---

[32] I. Shapiro and K. Tebeau, 'Introduction' in *After Apartheid: Reinventing South Africa?*, ed. I. Shapiro and K. Tebeau (Charlottesville and London: University of Virginia Press, 2011), pp. 1–18.

the ANC to agree to the adoption of a negotiated interim constitution.[33] The latter would set constraints on the substance of the final constitution, entrench a government of national unity for 5 years and ensure the legal continuity the government required. The negotiations resumed on a new basis and with renewed impetus as all now realized that there really was no other alternative to a negotiated settlement (if viewed positively) or elite compromise (if viewed with more scepticism).

The point though is not that the settlement or pact was somehow now inevitable, partly, of course, because at the time, during the negotiations, it clearly was not: violence was not only imminent, but broke out sporadically throughout the negotiations; and various events, particularly the assassination of Chris Hani on 10 April 1993, stretched it to breaking point. The main point is that various elements came together that made the main parties able not only to compromise but also cohere around a set of institutions and ways of conceiving them. The most important of these, and the one that could be said to underpin the possibility of the above-described concessions, was the fact that from the very outset of the negotiation process, the major political parties agreed that a democratic South Africa should be constructed on the basis of a justiciable constitution, articulated in terms of safeguarding the equal human rights of all South Africans. Three things follow from this. First, the constitution is the supreme law, binding all parts of the state including the legislative majority and making constitutional change possible only by means of amending the constitution itself, through special and very demanding procedures and a special majority of legislators. Second, a justiciable constitution empowers the judiciary to uphold the constitution, thus making not only the constitution but also, in effect, the constitutional court sovereign. Contrast this to a system in which parliament is sovereign, where courts are required to abide by the decisions of a political majority in parliament. 'Under constitutional supremacy, the courts are mandated to enforce the Constitution even to the point of striking down the decisions of the democratically elected legislature'.[34] Most importantly, the function of the courts under the system agreed upon by both parties is to uphold the rights guaranteed in the constitution against violation by the state or by private bodies. This basic agreement over what amounted to a fundamental change in the role of the courts and the place of law in the governance of South African society was only made possible by the underlying fact that both major

---

[33] Constitution of the Republic of South Africa, xv.
[34] Constitution of the Republic of South Africa, xvi.

parties were satisfied with the idea of human rights as the founding set of principles or lexicon for the interim constitution and then, ultimately, the final constitution.

Most importantly, therefore, the nature of the proposed new political order was the consequence of the fact that the two main parties were able to cohere around the language of human rights. Despite its history of vitriol against notions such as human rights, the NP quickly came to see that, within a democratic South Africa, the ANC would easily command majority support and thus a majority in parliament for some time to come. For the NP and those they represented, therefore, the language of human rights, inclusive of cultural and group rights as it is, enabled them to safeguard some of their interests, even under conditions of being in a permanent minority. The fact that parliament, and thus elected political representatives, would thereby be much less significant and powerful than in the regime they had created in 1948 was now of no concern to them; in fact, given the likely future scenario, all the better that parliament be severely constrained and weakened by a sovereign, human rights-based constitution. For the ANC, despite reservations regarding a number of rights within the eventual bill of rights, the language of rights in general and human rights in particular had been part of its lexicon since at least the Freedom Charter of 1955, if not even further back. That these two otherwise warring parties could cohere over the relatively abstract language of human rights may seem remarkable, until one remembers two highly significant global developments. First, the rapid growth in global power of the human rights discourse, at least ever since the adoption by the United Nations (UN) General Assembly on 10 December 1948 of the Universal Declaration of Human Rights. Second, that following, in particular, the two apartheid massacres at Sharpeville on 21 March 1960 and at Soweto on 16 June 1976, the anti-apartheid movement had not only become internationalized (and much of its power rested on this) but had, as a result, wholeheartedly embraced the discourse of human rights.[35] One of the co-authors of the Freedom Charter has stated unambiguously that the emphasis on human rights in the Freedom Charter is a direct consequence of the global currency of these notions at the time, and this emphasis was reiterated at the Morogoro Conference in April 1969 and again in the 1989 Harare Declaration that converted the vision of the Charter 'into a constitutional reality'.[36] And, of course, the eventual final constitution of 1996 is now the standard bearer for defenders of human rights all across the world.

---

[35] Dubow, *African National Congress* and Lodge, *Sharpeville*.
[36] B. Turok, *From the Freedom Charter to Polokwane*.

Thus, the *impasse* in military and political power between the two main parties, the end of the cold war, the internationalization of the anti-apartheid struggle and coherence around the language of human rights enabled an agreement. Together they enabled the negotiators to identify a set of interests and goals that most could agree on. Also, lest it be forgotten, by its very nature, the elite compromise had to satisfy the interests and reduce the fears of both sides and thus had to institutionalize forms of political power that safeguarded existing interests – that is, the interests of the elites during the process of negotiation – rather than enable a revolutionary shift of power or interests. In other words, for consensus of a kind to emerge, the settlement could not empower the previously disenfranchised too rapidly and at the direct expense of the previously advantaged. The human rights discourse did just that.

Although human rights safeguarded within a sovereign constitution may have helped ensure peaceful transition, it had a series of deleterious long-term effects on the prospects for real political freedom in South Africa. The human rights-based emphasis on settling a volatile *status quo* and the need to look backwards and find ways of resolving and healing the wrongs and injustices of the past have left South Africa with a macro-political and macroeconomic legacy that was unable to deal with its future. This is readily apparent in three centrally important components of the economy and polity ever since. First, a conservative and austere macroeconomic policy that prioritized stabilizing the mess of an economy handed over by the NP government and then, very slowly, a shift towards distribution of wealth by means of growth at the expense of radical redistribution of incomes and resources. (The dynamics of this and the associated response to public debt are discussed in full in Chapter 4.) Second, the form and substance of the new constitution, which in great detail manages to make constant reference to righting the wrongs of the past, safeguarding the existing rights of all across a deeply divided society, remove sovereignty from parliament and generates a series of extra-parliamentary checks and balances in the form of what have become known as the Chapter 9 institutions. Third is the structure and dynamics of a completely new electoral system, a party-list proportional representation system in place of the polar opposite Westminster first-past-the-post system tainted by its use under apartheid (as discussed in detail in Chapter 3).

The effect of these three structural decisions is an arrangement that leaves little or no room for everyday citizens to affect the manner in which the polity and economy is managed. Once they have voted, they have no means of calling political representatives to account as representatives are no longer bound to

a particular constituency and citizens elect parties, which determine who will
represent them – the latter is intended as ambiguous because, of course, under
this form of proportional representation, representatives represent the interest
of their parties and not those of the citizens or some subsection of the latter.
Economically, although citizens in democratic South Africa may have formal
rights to a plethora of goods, as articulated in the constitution, in order to realize
these rights they need the social and economic power that these formal rights
on their own cannot provide. This condition of reifying extreme inequality by
means of an institutional arrangement premised on formal equality (not, of
course, unique to South Africa) is exacerbated in South Africa by the perceived
need to use state resources and powers to generate quickly a 'black' middle class;
the most efficient means of doing so is the associated willing cooptation of the
existing 'white' economic elite. The result is that the spoils of the new state and
its associated markets have been retained in a very small numbers of hands, as is
spelled out in Chapters 2 and 4, in particular.

What follows from this on the ground in South Africa today is debilitating for
freedom as power in three ways. (Or, in other words, the effects on the ground
are that most South Africans remain dominated in one or all of the four ways
specified above.) First, even though the elite compromise generated a peaceful
outcome, the real material advantages of that peace were kept securely in the
hands of a new class of elites that very quickly closed shop on further entrants
and proceed to seek and secure rents for their privileged positions right across
the polity and economy, further exacerbated by an education system that fails to
generate sufficient numbers and quality of new entrants to challenge those who
now dominate in most spheres.[37] Second, this degree of elite compromise and
rent-seeking has given rise, quite understandably, to high levels of corruption
and highly distorted forms of patronage politics. Third, the *impasse* has not gone
away; it has only changed its spots, as it were. The new, mainly 'black' political
elite is periodically under threat of capital flight from an old, mainly 'white'
economic elite, upon whose capital part of the state's credibility rests; moreover,
the old economic elite is periodically under threat of the nationalization of
its wealth in general and its land, mineral resources and banks in particular.
A cold-war-style *impasse* – the *impasse* that gave rise and characterized the
negotiations between the NP and the ANC – has given way to an *impasse* based
on the relatively equal bargaining power of these two threats. The result is that

---

[37] R. de Kadt and C. Simkins, 'The Political Economy of Pervasive Rent-seeking', in *Thesis Eleven* 115 (April, 2013), pp. 112–126.

most, if not all, of the country's economic and political energies and institutions are focused on maintaining the equilibrium between these two extreme threats, and what follows from this is little movement on empowering and freeing the rest of the population and the fact that this majority does not constitute (and finds it very difficult to enter) either of these two groups and so its needs go unheard, unevaluated and unmet. I will return to these systemic problems of post-apartheid South Africa in greater detail in subsequent chapters, but it is worth noting here that their effect is to keep the majority either unrepresented or poorly represented in this incessant elite bargaining stalemate. Thus, taken together, what follows from this is that most South Africans are dominated in all the four ways stipulated earlier: they do not have the material resources, institutional access or requisite knowledge properly to identify, express, evaluate or meet their needs.

These forms of domination also explain the frequency of (often violent) protests against local-level corruption and the poor delivery of public services: in short, the majority of the population simply have no other voice, no other means of expressing their needs and the fact that they are being left unmet as a consequence of the elite pact that characterizes the institutions that were allegedly set up to respond to their needs. They remain dominated, but they do not have the institutional means to express their claims for greater freedom in legal and constructive ways; their only recourse is not only to protest but also to escalate the way in which they protest to such a level that they and their needs will be noticed by the ruling elites. Put differently, they have to be sufficiently destructive of the polity or the post-apartheid peace to make it in the interests of the elites to respond in some manner.

Most importantly, the human rights legal framework and structure of governance as secured by South Africa's sovereign constitution of 1996 actually disempower rather than empower South African citizens. Rather than furthering their freedom as power, it stops them from overcoming the four forms of domination that prevail. The reason it does this is because, first, rights are not processes; they are trumps. They stop processes. They predetermine interests; they reify interests in a pre-political fashion. Politics is all about processes, processes that identify, express, form, evaluate, prioritize and then meet needs, and these processes are best undertaken with as much participation and input by those whose needs will ultimately be met.[38] As understood here, at the very

---

[38] F. Fehér *et al.*, *The Dictatorship Over Needs* (Oxford: Basil Blackwell, 1983); Hamilton, *Needs*; Geuss and Hamilton, 'Human Rights'.

least, that will involve the power to determine who rules – or who represents the people or the various sub-groups thereof – the power to sanction who rules, and the power to be involved in the decisions they make regarding, in particular, macroeconomic policy. Human rights, moreover, are rough-hewn, they are crude legal functions that have to be relatively undifferentiated; however, politics is, or at least ought to be, all about something much more subtle, especially in extremely unequal or divided societies: the ability to differentiate between people and their needs and thus activate citizens, motivate them to demand successfully the various goods that will provide them with freedom as power. Human rights combined with an impotent parliament – an electoral system that empowers the majority party and little else – and conservative macroeconomic policy together block any attempt citizens may make to participate in politics or, at least, control their representatives. Finally, human rights are counterproductive to the goal of overcoming domination because they tend to give individual citizens with little or no control politically over what happens a sense of some kind of control. Even when I don't have control over my street, my city or my state, at least I feel as if I have some kind of control, I have a right to something-or-other. 'Rights under this aspect are the modern form of opiate for politically neutred populations.'[39] In other words, not only do human rights constitute one of the components of the complex of institutions that maintain domination in South Africa, they act to create the illusion of power, control and freedom where there is none or very little.

As Marx said of the Declaration of the Rights of Man and of the Citizen (1791 and 1793 versions), the radical constitution produced during the French Revolution,

> [i]t is curious that a nation that begins to liberate itself, to tear down all barriers between the various national groupings and to found a political community solemnly proclaims ... the privileges of egoistic man, separated from his fellow man and from the community ... This fact becomes even more curious if we consider that citizenship in the state, that the *political community*, is even reduced by the political emancipators to the status of a mere *means* for the preservation of these so-called human rights ... 'The *aim* of all *political associations* is the *preservation* of the natural and imprescriptible rights of man'. (Declaration of the Rights etc. of 1791, Art. 2) '*Government* is instituted to guarantee man the enjoyment of his natural and imprescriptible rights'. (Declaration etc. of 1793 Art. 1)[40]

---

[39] Geuss and Hamilton, 'Human Rights'.
[40] K. Marx, 'On the Jewish Question', in K. Marx, *Early Political Writings*, ed. J. O'Malley and R. A. Davis (Cambridge: Cambridge University Press, 1994 [1843]), pp. 45–46. Many thanks to James Furner for reminding me of this quote.

Written in 1843, this statement could have been written of South Africa two decades after the 'miracle' political liberation of her people.

Conclusion

The experience of South Africa over at least the last 60 years only reinforces the argument of the first half of this chapter regarding how best to understand political freedom: in terms of 'freedom is power'. This is the case for hopeful and deeply troubling reasons. The first reason is that political liberty is clearly still cherished very strongly in South Africa, as is the liberty to pursue private enjoyments. Political liberty is so important not only because it was only very recently and precariously achieved, but also because it needs to be constantly maintained and secured, and because without it, private independence will itself no longer be assured. The hopeful or uplifting characteristic of contemporary South Africa is that, given the historical proximity of liberation, some citizens still see this relationship with unwavering clarity and nerve. Like Machiavelli and others and as the experiences of many states throughout history show, they see that the attainment of political liberation is only one of a number of necessary conditions for individual political freedom. At the very least, citizens have to put in place and support institutions that maintain the form of regime that provides them with the array of necessary conditions for freedom.

However, the deeply troubling pervasive reason that further supports the importance of conceiving of freedom as power is that, as will be shown fully in the remaining three chapters, political freedom and the institutions that are supposed to maintain it can very easily be or become corrupted, even if formally they retain legitimacy, and thus fail not only to secure political freedom itself but also to provide the various other necessary conditions for individual independence and freedom. Contrary to the contemporary tendency to laud democracy and democratic institutions simply if and when they fulfil a set of formal conditions – periodic elections, free competition, free access to power, non-violent alternation of governing parties and so on – I maintain that the question of whether democracy as a form of regime secures freedom and is thus valuable is a substantive one, the answer to which lies in the extent to which any actual democracy enables the set of substantive powers and freedoms discussed in this chapter. However, South Africa has some way to go before it secures these substantive powers and freedoms for its citizens and this is because it has yet to properly secure both forms of liberty, that is, political liberty in the form of active and meaningful involvement in the agencies of one's political community and the degree of power necessary to live an independent and non-dependent life. Or, in other words, the majority of South Africans are still dominated in four debilitating ways. Despite, or partly because of, the promises of the Freedom Charter of 1955 and the Constitution of 1996, existing power relations in South Africa: (a) mislead most South Africans in their attempts to *identify* their needs; (b) ensure that they do not have the means or voice to *express* their needs, or have them properly represented by others; (c) disable meaningful *evaluation* of needs, as they have no real means to determine macroeconomic policy; *and* (d) constrain their capacity to meet their needs, as the needs and interests of an elite economic and political class determine most macro-political and macroeconomic decisions.

2

Quality of Life

There is little doubt that South Africa has come a very long way since the release of Nelson Mandela and the overthrow of apartheid. It has liberated its people from the shackles of a regime based on racial segregation, domination and oppression, it has successfully consolidated representative democracy, the rule of law is upheld by an independent judiciary and a highly progressive and laudable constitution, and it has (in the main) stabilized and grown its economy to an extent inconceivable during the late 1980s and the early 1990s. At least until 2008, South Africa had 14 years of uninterrupted growth – with rates exceeding 5% between 2004 and 2007. Gross Domestic Product (GDP) now stands at $600 billion, which puts South Africa in the same league as the Netherlands, Poland and Argentina. With only 6.5% of the population of sub-Saharan Africa, South Africa produces 37.3% of its GDP. Since 1994 the government has built close to three million houses; and more than 13 million people now receive social grants.[1]

These figures are corroborated by the latest census, which identifies a number of significant achievements.[2] The proportion of the 'black African' population with higher education more than doubled between 1996 and 2011 and those with no schooling more than halved during the same period (as did the overall proportion of those with no schooling). Over the past ten years, the average annual household income in South Africa more than doubled (up to R103 204 in 2011 from R48 385 in 2001, an increase of 113.3% in nominal terms). There has been a substantial increase in the percentage of households living in a formal dwelling as compared to traditional and informal dwellings: in 1996, 65.1% of households lived in formal dwellings, as compared to 77.6% in 2011; the percentage of households living in traditional dwellings almost halved (although the percentage of households living in informal dwellings decreased

---

[1] F. W. de Klerk, 'We Astounded the World and Will Do so Again', *The Times*, 13 February, 2010, p. 24.
[2] Statistics South Africa (SSA), Census 2011: Statistical Release (Revised)[online](2012), P0301.4. Available from: http://www.statssa.gov.za/publications/P03014/P030142011.pdf [accessed 25 May 2013].

by less than 3%, from 16.2% in 1996 to 13.6% in 2011). During the same period the percentage of households with access to piped water within their dwelling or yard increased from 60.8% to 73.4%. Finally, most impressively, the percentage of households that use electricity for lighting – that is, have been successfully connected to the national energy grid – rose from 58.2% in 1996 to 84.7% in 2011 and to 85% in 2012.[3]

Given the common consensus that access to housing, water and education combined with above-inflation income increases are not only necessary for the satisfaction of basic or vital human needs[4] but also that these are vital for helping to lift people out of poverty, this combination of economic stabilization and the introduction of various mechanisms to satisfy vital needs has been an unmitigated success story, particularly in terms of helping large swathes of the population escape conditions of *extreme* poverty. This is corroborated by a number of studies, including the General Household Surveys (GHS) 2001–2007, that show that although the record for the late 1990s is not as clear-cut, a sharp increase in pro-poor public expenditure on social assistance programmes did lead to a reduction in poverty.[5] Moreover, this is true when using a low poverty line (US$1 per capita per day, or R250 per capita per month) and a higher poverty line (US$1.5 per day, or R422 per capita per month): utilizing the former Bhorat and Van der Westhuizen found that the proportion of South Africans living in poverty fell from about 31% in 1995 to about 23% in 2005, and using the latter they found the rate fell, if a lot less dramatically, from about 52% to about 48%.[6] In other words, although ANC claims in the mid-2000s that the data shows that South Africans had 'never had it so good' and that it had laid the 'foundation for a better life for all' were clearly over-stated, the post-apartheid government has succeeded in reducing the proportion of the population living in conditions of extreme poverty, that is, the number of people with incomes below US$1 per day.[7]

---

[3]   Statistics South Africa (SSA), Census 2011, pp. 34, 41, 57, 59, 61; Statistics South Africa (SSA), General Household Survey 2012 (Revised Version)[online](2012), Statistics Release PO318. Available from: http://www.statssa.gov.za/Publications/P0318/P0318August2012.pdf [accessed 28 August 2013], p. 25.

[4]   On the overlap and distinction between the two, see L. Hamilton, *The Political Philosophy of Needs* (Cambridge: Cambridge University Press, 2003).

[5]   J. Seekings, 'Poverty and Inequality in South Africa, 1994–2007' in *After Apartheid: Reinventing South Africa?*, ed. I. Shapiro and K. Trebeau (Charlottesville: University of Virginia Press, 2011), pp. 27–28.

[6]   Cited in Seekings, 'Poverty and Inequality in South Africa', p. 27. The rand equivalents are adapted from Meth, who provides an elaborate analysis of the intricate complexities around the seemingly simple notion of low and high poverty lines. C. Meth, 'Half-measures Revisited: The ANC's Unemployment and Poverty Reduction Goals' in *Poverty and Policy in Post-Apartheid South Africa*, ed. H. Bhorat and R. Kanbur (Cape Town: HSRC Press, 2006), p. 400.

[7]   Seekings, 'Poverty and Inequality in South Africa', pp. 23–25.

In this chapter, I use various sources to assess the existing levels of poverty, inequality, unemployment and education in South Africa to provide a snapshot of the existing quality of life for most South Africans;[8] and, in so doing, I compare the current state of affairs to ten and twenty years back, at the end of three and half centuries of alien rule, first colonial of various forms and then legalized racism and oppression in the form of nearly half a decade of apartheid.

Poverty

The figures just quoted, however, mask a much deeper, systemic problem that the post-apartheid ANC government in South Africa has failed to address: not only the fact that levels of absolute poverty remain remarkably, stubbornly high for a relatively wealthy middle-income country of South Africa's stature, but also that the picture regarding poverty, inequality, education and unemployment when taken together is much, much bleaker. In fact, not only is it much bleaker than the portrait just sketched, it paints a grim depiction indeed of the fact that the various macroeconomic policies instituted over the last 20 years have, one after the other, failed to change the distorted socio-economic landscape inherited from apartheid South Africa.

As regards absolute poverty, according to the South African government, in 2007 the total number of people living in conditions of extreme poverty, that is, living on or below R250 per month or approximately US$1 per day, stood at just over 11 million individuals or 19% of the total population. The proportion of people living just above this extreme, that is, on or below R365 per month or US$1.5 per day, stood at 41%.[9] This general trend is corroborated by two further studies from a year earlier and a year later that provide evidence to show that between 30% and 40% of the population are unable adequately to meet their basic needs, 17.6% are illiterate, 43% experienced a food shortage and 10%

---

[8] For more on the relationship between poverty, inequality, education, freedom and quality of life, see A. Sen, *Commodities and Capabilities* (Amsterdam: North-Holland, 1985a); A. Sen, 'Well-being, Agency and Freedom: The Dewey Lectures 1984', in *Journal of Philosophy*, 82.4 (1985b), pp. 169–221; A. Sen, 'The Equality of What?', in *Liberty, Equality, and Law*, ed. S. M. McMurrin (Cambridge: Cambridge University Press, 1987a), pp. 137–162; A. Sen, *On Ethics and Economics* (Oxford: Basil Blackwell, 1987b); A. Sen, *Inequality Reexamined* (Oxford: Basil Clarendon Press, 1992); A. Sen, 'Positional Objectivity', in *Philosophy and Public Affairs*, 22 (1993), pp. 126-145; A. Sen, *Development as Freedom* (Oxford: Oxford University Press, 1999).

[9] The Presidency Republic of South Africa, Development Indicators 2008 [online](2008). Available from: http://www.info.gov.za/view/DownloadFileAction?id=84952 [accessed 9 July 2010], pp. 26–27.

experienced a food shortage *always* or *many times* in the 12 months ending May 2009.[10] If anything, as regards illiteracy in the work-age population, these figures constitute an underestimate, at least according to the latest census (2011) and the latest (2012) General Household Survey (GHS): the census records that more than one-fifth (20.8%) of individuals over the age of 20 years were functionally illiterate and GHS puts the 2012 figure at 16.5%.[11]

In terms of housing, between 2002 and 2008 there was a slight increase from 13.1% to 13.4% in the proportion of families living in informal dwellings and by 2012 there had been a further increase to 14.1%.[12] And, in the 12 months ending May 2009, 37% of South Africans experienced a shortage of clean water and 15% of South Africans experienced a shortage of clean water *always* or *many times*.[13] These figures for absolute poverty in South Africa are much lower as compared to other African countries such as Kenya, Senegal and Zambia, but this is like comparing apples and pears, as these countries are not *middle*-income countries and do not have anywhere near the levels of income, infrastructure, general development and GDP per capita as South Africa, however skewed its spread and efficacy is thanks to the extreme distortions of apartheid's legacy. Comparable poverty rates in Chile, Mexico, Indonesia, Jamaica, Malaysia and Tunisia, for example, have been much lower across this whole two-decade period.[14] Only Brazil matched South Africa in the 1990s,[15] but the former has since implemented highly successful poverty reduction programmes, which leaves South Africa now as the sole outlier in terms of absolute poverty in the *middle*-income country bracket.

Moreover, absolute income poverty is just one measure of welfare or well-being. As initiated by the groundbreaking ethical and economic work of Amartya

[10] Statistics South Africa (SSA), 2007/2008 Human Development Report, South Africa [online](2008). Available from: http://hdrstats.undp.org/countries/country_fact_sheets/cty_fs_ZAF.html [accessed 9 July 2010]; A. Leatt, 'Income Poverty in South Africa' [online]. Available from: http://www.ci.org.za/depts/ci/pubs/pdf/general/gauge2006/gauge2006_incomepoverty.pdf [accessed July 2010]; Poverty Net, Understanding Poverty and World Bank Poverty Report [online](2008). Available from: http://web.worldbank.org/WBSITE/EXTERNAL/TOPICS/EXTPOVERTY/EXTPA/0,,contentMDK:20153855~menuPK:435040~pagePK:148956~piPK:216618~theSitePK:430367,00.html [accessed 10 July 2010]; Afrobarometer, *Afrobarometer Briefing Paper No. 68* [online] (2009). Available from: http://www.afrobarometer.org/papers/AfrobriefNo68_21may09_newfinal.pdf [accessed 19 July 2010], pp. 5–6.
[11] Statistics South Africa (SSA), Census 2011; Statistics South Africa (SSA), General Household Survey 2012, p. 14.
[12] Statistics South Africa (SSA), General Household Survey July 2008 [online](2012). Available from: http://www.statssa.gov.za/publications/P0318/P0318July2008.pdf [accessed 8 July 2010], p. 5; Statistics South Africa (SSA), General Household Survey 2012, p.22.
[13] Afrobarometer, *Afrobarometer Briefing Paper No. 68*, p. 6.
[14] Seekings, 'Poverty and Inequality in South Africa', p. 21.
[15] United Nations Development Programme (UNDP), *Human Development Report 1999* (Geneva: United Nations Development Programme, 1999).

Sen,[16] the Human Development Index (HDI) is a broader measure of quality of life, reported in the UNDP's annual *Human Development Report (HDR)*. The HDI comprises three components: an 'educational attainment index', constructed out of adult literacy rates and gross school enrolment rates; a 'life expectancy index', derived from data on life expectancy at birth; and an index of Gross National Income (GNI) per capita expressed in constant 2005 international dollars converted using purchasing power parity (PPP) rates.[17] The first thing to note about this measure across time is that South Africa's absolute HDI has been more or less the same ever since 1990, when it was 0.621, up until the latest assessment (2012), when it was 0.629,[18] but that this has meant a steady drop in its global ranking relative to the HDI of other countries from 90 in 1994 to 125 in 2007 and 121 in 2012. Disaggregating further, these indicators show that, with the exception of 1999, there was a sharp drop off in ranking from 1994 until 2002, when South Africa reached a global ranking of 119, a position it has more or less stabilized at, slipping as low as 125th in 2006.[19] This is out of a total number of 187 countries, and these stabilized low rankings for South Africa put it in the lower half of what the *HDR* calls 'medium human development', the third of four categories, on a par with countries such as Indonesia, which has surged up the rankings over the last two decades, and surrounded by countries such as Kyrgyzstan and Viet Nam, with much lower GDP per capita. Most of the other *middle*-income countries, categorized in terms of GDP per capita, are much higher up on the *HDR* rankings in the 'high human development category', for example, Poland (39th), Chile (40th) and even South Africa's erstwhile highly unequal 'partner in crime', Brazil (85th).

This rapid decline in South Africa's absolute and relative HDI is due, in major part, to the rapid decline in life expectancy in South Africa. One of the important

---

[16] A. Sen, *Collective Choice and Social Welfare* (San Francisco: Holden Day, 1970); A. Sen, *Poverty and Famines: An Essay on Entitlement and Deprivation* (Oxford: Clarendon Press, 1981); Sen, *Commodities and Capabilities*; Sen, 'Well-being, Agency and Freedom'; Sen, 'The Equality of What?'; Sen, *On Ethics and Economics*; Sen, *Inequality Reexamined*; Sen, 'Positional Objectivity'; Sen, *Development as Freedom*.

[17] United Nations Development Programme (UNDP), *Human Development Report 2013: The Rise of The South: Human Progress in a Diverse World: Explanatory Note on 2013 HDI Composite Indices: South Africa* [online] (Geneva: United Nations Development Programme, 2013b). Available from: http://hdrstats.undp.org/images/explanations/ZAF.pdf [accessed 26 August 2013].

[18] United Nations Development Programme (UNDP), *Human Development Report 2013: The Rise of The South: Human Progress in a Diverse World* [online] (Geneva: United Nations Development Programme: 2013a). Available from http://hdr.undp.org/en/media/HDR_2013_EN_complete.pdf [accessed 23 August 2013], p.149; United Nations Development Programme (UNDP), *Human Development Report 2013: The Rise of The South: Human Progress in a Diverse World: Explanatory Note on 2013 HDI Composite Indices: South Africa* [online].

[19] Seekings, 'Poverty and Inequality in South Africa', pp. 30–31; United Nations Development Programme (UNDP), *Human Development Report 2013: The Rise of The South: Human Progress in a Diverse World* [online] p. 149.

consequences of absolute poverty is the direct effects it has on quality of life and, ultimately, on rates of mortality. According to the latest HDI, in 2012 in South Africa life expectancy at birth was 53.4 years, and this following a recent rise since 2005, when it was just over 50 years.[20] Moreover, as is now common knowledge, in the case of South Africa this very low figure has been heavily influenced by the devastating effects of the HIV/AIDS pandemic, thanks in significant degree to the effects of the Thabo Mbeki-led ANC government denial regarding the scientific evidence for the link between HIV and AIDS and their subsequent very slow roll-out of a national treatment campaign. By 2010, AIDS reduced life expectancy at birth in South Africa by almost 20 years: without AIDS it would have been 68 years; with AIDS and AIDS denialism, it was 52.2 years.[21] Besides the human tragedy of this very poor political judgement and associated lack of accountability that allowed it to continue more or less unchallenged for so long, if anything, it has rolled back decades of development,[22] generating in many areas a lost generation: child-headed households, significantly lowered household income, the need therefore to seek employment and thus leave formal education at a younger age than would otherwise be the case, and so on. As regards general health, according to the UNDP report of 2007–2008, 31% of South Africans face the probability of not surviving past the age of 50, which is a measure of the poor state of healthcare provision, lack of universal access to existing provision, the consequences of the HIV/AIDS pandemic and the effects of South Africa's political representatives' lack of accountability. (As I argue in the next chapter, the latter is due to the nature of its macro-political institutional structure.) Child mortality rates have not improved in South Africa since 1990. Finally, 'black' South Africans experience poverty at over three times the rate of 'white' and 'indian' respondents.[23]

This generally very parlous state of affairs regarding poverty is corroborated overall by a new UNDP index called the Multidimensional Poverty Index (MPI), introduced in 2010, which identifies multiple deprivations in education,

[20] United Nations Development Programme (UNDP), *Human Development Report 2013: The Rise of The South: Human Progress in a Diverse World: Explanatory Note on 2013 HDI Composite Indices: South Africa* [online].

[21] Seekings, 'Poverty and Inequality in South Africa', p. 31 – claims there corrected in light of United Nations Development Programme (UNDP), *Human Development Report 2013: The Rise of The South: Human Progress in a Diverse World: Explanatory Note on 2013 HDI Composite Indices: South Africa* [online].

[22] N. Nattrass, 'AIDS and Human Security in Southern Africa', in *Social Dynamics*, 28.1 (2002), pp. 1–19; United Nations Development Programme (UNDP), *Human Development Report 2013: The Rise of The South: Human Progress in a Diverse World: Explanatory Note on 2013 HDI Composite Indices: South Africa* [online].

[23] Afrobarometer, *Afrobarometer Briefing Paper No. 68* [online] p. 8.

health and standard of living, providing a means of assessing whether an entire household (i.e. everyone in it) is either multidimensionally poor or *vulnerable* to or at risk of becoming multidimensionally poor. In South Africa's case the latest relevant figures were collected in 2008, when 13.4% of the population lived in multidimensional poverty and a further 22.2% were vulnerable to multiple deprivations. It follows that at least 35.6% of South Africa's population are either deprived across all dimensions, some dimensions or are at severe risk of becoming so. The most outstanding feature of these measures, however, is the disparity between South Africa's GNI per capita ($9,594) and its HDI and MPI.[24] Taken alone, South Africa's GNI per capita would place it squarely within the *middle*-income category and puts it on a par with most of the countries in the *HDR's* 'High Human Development' category, but its HDI and MPI indicators place it much further down the rankings. More specific HDI comparison is useful too: Brazil, for example, has a GNI per capita ($10, 152) very similar to that of South Africa and yet ranks 85th, not to mention Montenegro (GNI per capita of $10,471 and ranked 52nd) or the fact that Cuba (59th), Grenada (63rd), Serbia (64th), Peru (77th), Macedonia (78th), Ukraine (78th) and all the other countries bar five that are ranked between Ukraine and South Africa all have a GNI per capita lower than South Africa, in some cases significantly lower. This discrepancy between GNI per capita rank and HDI rank is also calculated in the *HDR*, and South Africa has the infamy of scoring –42, the 4th worse score on the entire index of 187 countries.[25] This points to one of the main causes not only of poverty in South Africa but also of the lack of freedom that still prevails in South Africa: the extreme inequality it has failed to eradicate.

Inequality

South Africa is one of the most unequal societies on earth. The Gini coefficient is a widely accepted summary measure of income (or wealth) inequality that ranges from zero (perfect equality in the distribution of income or wealth) to one (perfect inequality in the distribution of income or wealth). South Africa had a Gini coefficient of 0.72, the world's highest. This unequal distribution means that large parts of the South African population are unable to benefit

[24] United Nations Development Programme (UNDP), *Human Development Report 2013: The Rise of The South: Human Progress in a Diverse World* [online], p. 145.
[25] United Nations Development Programme (UNDP), *Human Development Report 2013*, pp. 144–147.

equally from economic growth: for example, in 2008 the poorest 40% of households, which comprise 55% of the South African population, were responsible for just below 10% of national consumption expenditure, whilst the poorest 10% of households (17% of the population) were only responsible for 2% of consumption. This is in stark contrast to the richest 10% of households (which account for only 6% of the population) that are responsible for 45% of consumption.[26] The World Bank's latest figures, from 2009, corroborate this reality of extreme inequality: the poorest 10% of population were responsible for only 1% of consumption, whereas the richest 10% of the population was responsible for 52% of consumption.[27]

Moreover, since 1996, despite some inroads into eradicating some components of extreme poverty, as outlined in the previous section, South Africa has become more unequal, not less unequal. Leibbrandt's calculations using the 1995 and 2000 Income and Expenditure Surveys show that the Gini coefficient for household per capita income rose by five percentage points over five years, from 0.65 to 0.7. The 1996 and 2001 population census data corroborate this finding nearly perfectly.[28] These not only corroborate the findings about the current states of affairs regarding inequality, but also show that matters have only further worsened since 1996. Moreover, as Seekings argues, the Gini coefficient may even underestimate the degree of inequality in contemporary South Africa as it is reportedly less sensitive to changes at either end of the income distribution and more sensitive to changes in the middle. 'South Africa's rich are unusually rich and South Africa's poor are exceptionally poor, even relative to other unequal societies. If the poor are getting relatively poorer, therefore, the Gini coefficient shows less change than alternative measures of distribution, such as the mean logarithmic deviation.'[29]

There has also been some recent dispute regarding the way in which the Gini coefficient is calculated, with a study in 2010 suggesting that it fails to take into account sufficiently the impact of government policies such as social grants

[26] P. Armstrong, B. Lekezwa and K. Siebrits, 'Poverty in South Africa: A Profile based on Recent Household Surveys' [online] (University of Stellenbosch, 2008). Available from: http://www.ekon.sun.ac.za/wpapers/2008/wp042008/wp-04-2008.pdf [accessed 20 July 2010] cf. The Presidency Republic of South Africa, Development Indicators 2008 [online], p. 25.

[27] World Bank, 2013 People: World Development Indicators: Distribution of Income or Consumption [online](2012). Available from: http://wdi.worldbank.org/table/2.9 [accessed 27 August 2013].

[28] J. Seekings, N. Nattrass and M. V. Leibbrandt, *Income Inequality After Apartheid* (University of Cape Town Centre for Social Science Research: Southern Africa Labour and Development Research Unit, 2004) cited in Seekings, 'Poverty and Inequality in South Africa', p. 28.

[29] Seekings, 'Poverty and Inequality in South Africa, 1994–2007', p. 29, citing J. Hoogeveen and B. Özler, 'Poverty and Inequality in Post-apartheid South Africa', in *Poverty and Policy in Post-Apartheid South Africa*, p. 72.

and free services, amongst others; social grants, in particular, have seen a sharp increase in uptake, with 12.7% of the population in 2002 as compared to 29.6% of the population in 2012 benefitting as individuals from social grants of one form or another. Concurrently, the percentage of households that received at least one grant increased from 29.9% in 2003 to 45.3% in 2009, before declining slightly to 43.6% in 2012.[30] The 2010 study found that when the income from social grants and free services was included in the calculation, the figure for South Africa drops to 0.61.[31] Even if this is correct, however, which many contest, this figure is not very far from the Gini index provided by both the latest *HDR* and the World Bank of 63.1 or an equivalent Gini coefficient of 0.63; more importantly, even this lowered figure corroborates that South Africa is one of the most unequal, if not the most unequal place on earth – compare South Africa's figure to that of Egypt (0.31), India (0.33), Indonesia (0.34), Russia (0.4), Paraguay (0.52) and Brazil (0.55).[32]

There is little doubt, therefore, that even if South African government intervention is beginning to eradicate extreme poverty, the overall picture regarding inequality is much gloomier: contrary to what many may assume following the end of apartheid and the election into power of a supposedly pro-poor party, the ANC, since 1994 South Africa has become more unequal not less unequal. *The World Top Incomes Database* corroborates this picture of increasing inequality in South Africa. This database and associated studies produce time-series analysis of the top incomes within countries not by reference to household surveys and other subjective information, whose veracity many have questioned, but objective data taken from annual tax submission statistics provided by the administration of tax revenues, in the case of South Africa by the South African Revenue Services. These figures indicate there is little doubt that South Africa is becoming more and more unequal. To take just one example from the study, in 2002 in South Africa those in the top 5% of income prior to tax shared 34.36% of the total income, and this has risen steadily until 2010 (the latest year that figures are available for) to 38.19% of the total income.[33]

---

[30] Statistics South Africa (SSA), General Household Survey 2012 [online], pp. 2, 19–20.
[31] L. Donnelly, 'Welfare Could Be Gini in the Bottle', *Mail &Guardian*, 10 May 2013.
[32] United Nations Development Programme (UNDP), *Human Development Report 2013: The Rise of The South: Human Progress in a Diverse World* [online]; World Bank, 2013 People: World Development Indicators: Distribution of Income or Consumption [online]; Donnelly, 'Welfare Could Be Gini in the Bottle.'
[33] F. Alvaredo, A. B. Atkinson, T. Piketty and E. Saez, *The World Top Incomes Database* [online](2012). Available from: http://topincomes.g-mond.parisschoolofeconomics.eu/#Database [accessed 28 August 2013], database South Africa.

Education and unemployment

In line with the moderate success regarding governmental response to extreme
poverty and the provision for vital needs, there has been some success since
1996 in reducing the proportion of the population without any schooling at
all. As the 2011 Census indicates, the proportion of persons aged 20 years
who have no schooling halved from 19.1% in 1996 to 8.6% in 2011; moreover,
according to the latest General Household Survey, by 2012 this percentage had
been further reduced to 5.8%, although the latter figure is noted as probably an
underestimate.[34] Further disaggregated, the census indicates a marked impact
on one of the previously disadvantaged groups, 'black African', improving
school attendance markedly for this group: from 24.0% of this group receiving
no schooling in 1996 to 10.5% in 2011, as compared to, for example, very
little change in the 'white' population's figures, an improvement from 1.1%
receiving no schooling in 1996 to 0.6% in 2011. Moreover, at the higher
end, there has been significant improvement in the inclusion of the 'black
African' population in the higher education system, with more than double
the proportion of persons with higher education between 1996 and 2011, an
increase of 3.6% to 8.3%.[35]

These improvements at the level of basic education and the increases for
the previously highly disadvantaged 'black African' population, however, mask
a generally very troubling state of affairs regarding education in South Africa,
especially regarding its capacities and outputs in terms of training its population
to be critical and employable citizens. For example, although the percentage of
persons aged 5–24 years attending a school in 2011 was as high as 93%, the
percentage attending a technikon or university was a staggeringly low 3% of this
population. Moreover, there has been very little increase in this proportion since
the end of apartheid: in 1996 7.1% of persons aged 20 years and older were able
to claim 'higher education' as their highest level of educational attainment; by
2011 this had only increased to 11.8%.[36] Even more startling for this vital process
of creating critical, literate and skilled citizens is the fact that between 2001 and
2011 there was a *decrease* in the proportion of persons aged 20 years and above
choosing to study the natural sciences, humanities and social sciences at the

---

[34] Statistics South Africa (SSA), General Household Survey 2012 [online], p.12.
[35] Statistics South Africa (SSA), Census 2011; Statistics South Africa (SSA), General Household Survey
      2012 [online], pp. 33–34.
[36] Statistics South Africa (SSA), Census 2011, p. 33.

tertiary level: in the natural sciences from 2.35% to 1.9%, in the humanities from 0.95% to 0.6% and in the social sciences from 6.0% to 4.95%.[37]

There is little dispute that South Africa's education system is systematically flawed, but comparisons with education systems and results in other countries really bring this reality into sharp relief. A recent World Economic Forum (WEF) Global Information Technology Report 2013 ranks South Africa's maths and science education second-last in the world, only ahead of Yemen. Furthermore, across all disciplines it ranks the quality of South Africa's education system 140th of 144 countries and internet access at schools 111th of 143 countries.[38] South African pupils routinely perform very badly in standardized international benchmarking tests (especially in mathematics), often ranking behind less-developed African countries.[39] It is no wonder that, according to the 2010 General Household Survey, although 98% of children between the ages of 7 and 15 years (the compulsory age range) are enrolled in schools, and that of every 100 pupils who start in Grade 1, about 94 reach Grade 9, dropout rates increase sharply in the 3-year senior secondary school phase – of every 100 starting Grade 10, fewer than 60 write the National Senior Certificate; and dropout rates increase *very* sharply subsequently in tertiary education – about half of those who enrol for degrees complete them and about 40% of those enrolling for diplomas do the same.[40] This is a consequence of an extremely unhealthy mix of post-apartheid educational policy that reacted against the authoritarian and rote learning characteristics of apartheid education policy, opting for progressive policy, learner creativity, tests and examinations by portfolios of work, group work as against competitive individualism and so on, but without the necessary training for those who were to introduce the new curriculum – the teachers themselves – coupled with very poor and often non-existent accountability structures in schools. The result, as studies consistently show, is low time on task and low cognitive effort made by teachers and learners alike.[41] In short, the result is a low-quality mass schooling system that fails to prepare learners for tertiary education or

---

[37] Statistics South Africa (SSA), Census 2011, p. 37, averages created from disaggregated gender difference.

[38] E. Pickwoth, 'Joint Initiative to Foster Education Reform', *Business Day*, 2 August 2013, p. 4.

[39] R. de Kadt and C. Simkins, 'The Political Economy of Pervasive Rent-seeking', *Thesis Eleven*, 115 (2013), p. 117.

[40] Statistics South Africa (SSA), General Household Survey 2010 (Revised Version), Statistics Release PO318, (Pretoria: Statistics South Africa, 2010b); de Kadt and Simkins, 'The Political Economy of Pervasive Rent-seeking' Corroborated by Statistics South Africa (SSA), General Household Survey 2012 [online], p.12.

[41] de Kadt and Simkins, 'The Political Economy of Pervasive Rent-seeking'.

employment and a tertiary education sector that has stagnated and is unable to provide the kind of quality or quantity of graduates necessary for the growing the economy and critical citizenship. Needless to say the likelihood of sustained growth and associated mechanisms for overcoming inequality and poverty depend on an educational system that can produce many more and many better qualified graduates. Moreover, as argued in de Kadt and Simkins, the filtering that takes place in secondary education and higher education means that those with a university qualification command high returns in the labour market and suffer markedly less unemployment than others.[42] These few can therefore seek and charge high rents for their skills, which impacts negatively on an already critical and unsustainable level of unemployment in South Africa.

Since 1994 any systemic attempts that have been made to alleviate absolute levels of poverty and unemployment and the extent of inequality have failed dismally. In fact in some instances conditions have worsened. Strict, official unemployment, for example, increased from 20% to 25.5% from 1994 to 2007[43]; as of 2011 matters had either worsened significantly if the census is your benchmark – 29.8% – or they have stabilized if the 2011 4th quarter results of the Quarterly Labour Force Survey (QLFS) are correct.[44] Depending on your source, over the last ten years or so there have been small fluctuations during different annual quarters but up until the present, approximately 25% of the population have been officially unemployed: according to Statistics South Africa, the latest figure stands at 25.2% of the population.[45] It is important to note, moreover, that this strict, official definition of unemployment does not include discouraged work seekers. These are people who are able and willing to work, but have given up any hope of finding employment. In other words the real, expanded figure regarding the percentage of unemployed is likely to be much higher, anywhere between 30 and 40% of the population; the 2011 census gives it as exactly 40% and the 4th quarter QLFS of 2011 as 35.4%.[46] Moreover, the highest rates of unemployment are found amongst young adults, those between the ages of 18 and 24 years. According to the census of 2011, a staggering

[42] de Kadt and Simkins, 'The Political Economy of Pervasive Rent-seeking'.
[43] South African Institute of Race Relations, Unemployment and Poverty: An Overview 28th November 2008 [online](2008). Available from: http://www.sairr.org.za/sairr-today/news_item.2008-11-28.9488661622/?searchterm=poverty%20statistics [accessed 5 July 2010].
[44] Statistics South Africa (SSA), Census 2011.
[45] Statistics South Africa (SSA), Quarterly Labour Force Survey: Quarter 1, 2013, Statistical Release P0211 [online](2013). Available from: http://www.statssa.gov.za/publications/P0211/P02111stQuarter2013.pdf [accessed 28 August 2013], p. xiv.
[46] Statistics South Africa (SSA), Census 2011.

48.6% of this age group is unemployed as calculated officially (i.e. not including discouraged work seekers) and an even more troubling 59.1% of this group is unemployed according to the expanded calculation (that includes discouraged work seekers).[47] This is a very worrying trend for the future of South Africa. In some countries this is offset by a large and efficient tertiary education sector that keeps this cohort in education and trains them for skilled jobs in the future. In South Africa the situation is bleak indeed: currently only 16% of those eligible for tertiary education find places in existing institutions of tertiary education; and, even more worryingly, of the 2.8 million South Africans between the ages of 18 and 24 years who in 2007 were not in employment, education and training, two million (71%) had not achieved grade 12 (final school year), and of these 0.5 million (18%) had not progressed beyond primary school.[48] And things have worsened since: towards the end of 2013, it looks as if almost a million school dropouts eligible for university entrance will *not* find places in universities and will thus end up in job queues; job queues that lead nowhere. The economy is shedding jobs and these school dropouts will constitute another million job seekers in a situation in which '3.5 million young people between the ages of 15 and 24 in the first quarter of 2013 were not absorbed into employment, education or training'.[49]

In other words, there is a compounding effect on unemployment. The economy and its macroeconomic masters are not even able to keep unemployment stable. The economy cannot even nearly absorb new work-seekers, let alone those already searching (not to mention those who have given up looking). Moreover, even if the economy were somehow to begin creating jobs, it is not clear whether those out of work would even be able to fill these positions, unless the jobs that were created all required unskilled labour, not exactly the recipe for enabling the reduction of poverty, inequality and unemployment in a middle-income country. Moreover, as if the current state of affairs was not bad enough, these figures for this age group make any realistic observer of South Africa gloomy regarding the possibility of reducing poverty, inequality and unemployment in South Africa's medium-term future. As I argue in the subsequent three chapters, much will depend on reorienting South Africa's macroeconomic, macro-political and educational institutions and practices.

---

[47] Statistics South Africa (SSA), Census 2011.

[48] M. Metcalfe, 'Mistakes We Cannot Make Again', *Mail & Guardian*, 3 to 9 September 2010.

[49] Minister for Higher Education and Training, Blade Nzimande, quoted in N. Mtshali, 'Universities Unable to Satisfy Demand for Places: Despite New Measures and New Universities, Almost a Million Matriculants Will End Up in Job Queues', *The Star*, 3 September 2013.

The health and freedom of the South African polity

As is apparent from the figures regarding poverty, inequality, health, education and unemployment in the previous sections, in and of itself poverty has dire effects on the well-being, life expectancy, general health and education of a large proportion of South Africa's population. Under current economic conditions a life trapped in a cycle of poverty is a life without power and thus a life without freedom across all four dimensions discussed in Chapter 1: without the financial means to satisfy properly my vital needs, I do not have the power to do or be as I would otherwise do or be (*in extremis* my situation *forces* me to act in certain ways in order often to stave off starvation, but even above that floor, if all my resources are directed towards the satisfaction of my vital needs, I have no surplus to use for my empowerment); nor do I have the time, education or power to determine who represents me, to take part in actively resisting the norms and practices of my society or to control those representatives that determine my economic environment.

However, the effects on power and freedom of absolute poverty are only exacerbated and exaggerated when they occur alongside extreme inequality, as is the case in South Africa. The very high levels of inequality in South Africa not only mean that a large proportion of the population struggle or are unable to meet their vital needs and thus enact the power necessary for freedom, they also skew the relative power and thus freedom of different sectors of society. I will elaborate on only two here. First, relatively poor citizens are left out of the economic loop in two ways: (a) they fail to prosper from a generally prosperous economy; and (b) they therefore have relatively little or no means of influencing their political and economic representatives, in particular with regard to the macroeconomic decisions that will affect whether or not they could be free and active economic agents in the future. They therefore become trapped in a cycle of less and less freedom. In contrast, the relatively affluent not only benefit directly from any positive national economic outcomes, they are also able to determine their future prospects by dint of their greater influence over macroeconomic policy, as a consequence of not only their greater purchasing power but also their direct and indirect links to policymakers (see Chapters 3 and 4).

However, the relatively wealthy are not exempt from the negative effects of high levels of inequality. They too are adversely affected in a number of ways. These are varied in number and kind but all have the effect of disempowering citizens and thus making them less free. South Africa's high levels of inequality give rise to a very high incidence of social ills that affect everyone, even the most wealthy and protected. It is not just the poor and deprived in isolation who suffer from the effects of inequality, but also the bulk of the population. In the most extreme and direct way, this is felt in the form of crime in general and violent crime in particular. Although the poor in South Africa are often the victims of crime, and as regards certain forms of crime, such as rape and murder, this is overwhelmingly the case, in no way whatsoever are the wealthy free from violent crime. In fact, they are often specifically targeted as a result of their wealth – armed robbery in South Africa occurs at very high levels in seemingly highly protected, wealthy suburbs and neighbourhoods. For example, Sandton, in Johannesburg, one of the wealthiest suburbs in South Africa, had the most cases of house robberies in the country during 2009–2010.[50] National crime statistics for 2008–2009 show a recent surge in house robberies (an increase of 27%), an overall increase in crime in general, and a slight drop in the murder rate; but despite the latter it is still the case that in South Africa about 50 people are murdered a day – slightly more than in the USA, which has six times South Africa's 50-million population.[51] In 2009–2010 there was a slight decline in murders, hijackings and sex crimes, while house and business robberies increased again.[52] Moreover, there is much evidence in South Africa and across the world that there is a direct and robust causal relation between high levels of inequality and crime.[53]

However, the severe social damage caused by inequality does not stop at violent crime. The high levels of inequality in South Africa also cause less direct, if equally damaging, effects on the whole population. These take the form of general stress, mutual distrust, conflict, violence, bad health, short lives, mental illness and low productivity. The lived experience in South Africa further bolsters some relatively new literature on the effects of inequality on the general health of

---

[50] The Star, '"Still too many murders": Experts Voice Caution as Major-crime Stats Show Decline', *The Star*, 10 September 2010.

[51] Mail & Guardian, 2009. 'SA Murder Rate Drops Slightly, Overall Crime up', *Mail & Guardian*, 22 September 2010; South African Police Service, South African Government Crime Statistics, 2009 [online](2009). Available from: http://www.saps.gov.za/statistics/reports/crimestats/2009/crime_stats.htm [accessed 5 July 2010].

[52] The Star, '"Still too many murders"'.

[53] R. G. Wilkinson, *The Impact of Inequality: How to Make Sick Societies Healthier* (London: Routledge, 2005); R. G. Wilkinson and K. Pickett, *The Spirit Level: Why More Equal Societies Almost All Do Better* (London: Allen Lane, 2009) *cf.* South African Police Service, 'Address by Minister of Police, Nathi Mthethwa, Deputy Minister Fikile Mbalula and Police Commissioner Bheki Cele to the members of the National Press Club' [online](2010). Available from: http://www.saps.gov.za/_dynamicModules/internetSite/newsBuild.asp?myURL=938 [accessed 15 July 2010]; Time Live, 'Cele Points Finger at "Nigerians in Sandton"', *Times Live*, 7 December 2009.

populations. Despite the incredible success of South Africa's relatively non-violent transformation and the rapidity with which many of its citizens have embraced Mandela's clarion call for the creation of a 'rainbow nation', the persistent high levels of material inequality make the wealthy, in particular, very distrustful of the poor, very protective of their precarious positions of relative wealth and often plagued by high levels of fear regarding their own and their family's health, safety and security. In this way and others, inequality breeds stress across the full spectrum of society, not just among the downtrodden, and this leads to a high incidence of syndromes such as depression, phobias of different sorts and basic anxiety. For example, incidents of mental illness are 500% higher across the whole population spectrum in the most unequal societies than in the most equal ones.[54] If these and other studies are correct – that there is a direct causal link between inequality and poor health, that is, mental and physical illness – there is little doubt that there exists a causal relation between high levels of inequality and power. If one is consistently having to struggle against poor health, one will accordingly lack the power to do or be as one would otherwise do or be, to take part in the selection and control of one's representatives and to resist the norms of one's society. It follows, therefore, that if one conceives of freedom in terms of power, the high levels of inequality experienced in South Africa severely curtail the freedom of all of its citizens. The second way therefore in which inequality and related problems associated with high levels of unemployment and a very poor educational system skew societal power relations and thus undermine the freedom as power of most of the population is through these causal links between inequality, crime, fear, mental and physical illness and thus freedom as power. It is not for nothing that many people in South Africa often speak about how important it is to be 'free from fear'.

In sum, then, given the levels of poverty, inequality, unemployment and poor education in South Africa, a large proportion of the population are faced with a continuous struggle to meet their vital needs and thus do not have the time or power to be free, and only a relatively small proportion of South Africans are able to act as they would otherwise choose or, more ambitiously, with the power to influence South Africa's macroeconomic policy. However, under the conditions prevalent in South Africa today, even these relatively powerful individuals lack freedom as a consequence of being constrained by crime, the fear of crime and the associated phobias and anxieties. A cycle of poverty for some when associated with high levels of inequality and unemployment has become a cycle of less and less freedom for all.

---

[54] Wilkinson, *The Impact of Inequality*; Wilkinson and Pickett, *The Spirit Level*.

Freedom's indivisibility

All South Africans lack freedom, even the economic and political elites, though, of course, the degree to which they lack it is significantly less than the impoverished, unemployed and poorly educated majority. As regards certain specific actions and indicators, such as life expectancy, nutrition, security, power of representatives and so on, members of the elite are freer than their impoverished and dominated fellow citizens. However, the very fact of the latter's states of domination undermines freedom for all South Africans, even the most opulent, lucky, malfeasant or hard-working elites. This is the case partly for reasons related to the famous claims made by Rousseau, Hegel, Marx and Mandela[55] regarding the fact that freedom depends on liberating the 'master and the slave', the 'oppressor and the oppressed' or, in Mandela's own words,

> [f]reedom is indivisible; the chains on any one of my people were the chains on all of them; the chains on all of my people were the chains on me ... the oppressor must be liberated just as surely as the oppressed ... The oppressed and the oppressor alike are robbed of their humanity.[56]

Although at the start of this quote he is describing conditions under apartheid, at the end he is clear that even following liberation from apartheid that statuses of 'oppressed' and 'oppressor' continued and would continue until real freedom for all was created. Under current conditions of political liberation in South Africa, it is better to see this not in terms of the direct oppression of one individual or group by another, but in terms of domination: the fact that the stagnation or worsening of economic and political conditions generates resilient states of domination that cause lack of freedom as power for all.

As I argued in Chapter 1, states of domination are characterized by power relations that block or fail to empower individuals in their attempts to determine and satisfy their needs. This can take various forms. Existing power relations can: (a) mislead me in my attempts to *identify* my needs; (b) ensure that I do not have the means or voice to *express* my needs; (c) disable meaningful *evaluation* of needs; and (d) constrain the capacity to *meet* needs. If we combine

---

[55] J-J. Rousseau, *The Social Contract*, in J-J. Rousseau, *The Social Contract and Other Later Political Writings*, ed. V. Gourevitch (Cambridge: Cambridge University Press, 1997 [1762]), pp. 39–152; G. W. F. Hegel, *Phenomenology of Spirit*, trans. A. V. Miller, foreword J. N. Findlay (Oxford: Oxford University Press, 1977 [1807]); K. Marx. *The Communist Manifesto*, introduced G. Stedman-Jones (London: Penguin, 2002 [1848]); N. Mandela, *Long Walk to Freedom: The Autobiography of Nelson Mandela* (Johannesburg: Macdonald Purnell, 1995).

[56] Mandela, *Freedom*, pp. 616–617.

the corrupt and distorted patronage politics of post-apartheid South Africa, which are partly a consequence of an unfortunate elite compromise, with the current conditions of poverty, inequality, unemployment, poor education and high levels of crime, it is easy to see that most South Africans are dominated in at least one of these ways. This will become even more apparent in the subsequent two chapters. My point is that although South Africans no longer live under conditions of intentional, direct oppression of one individual or group by another, it does not follow from this that they are now free and nor does it follow that they are now best placed to conceive of freedom in purely individualistic or atomistic terms. Various forms of domination still pervade South Africa and, as a result, our individual freedom and its lack and that of our fellow citizens are indivisible.

Our freedom depends on the freedom of others in the sense that we live in complex, interdependent modern states, within which our power to do as we would like, to conform or transgress and to determine who governs and how they do so, especially with regard to economic policy, depend ultimately on the *power* of all citizens across the four domains outlined in Chapter 1. Freedom is possible only when all citizens are able and willing to exercise their powers across all four of these dimensions of freedom as power. Without these substantive political and economic achievements and ideals, even if some citizens have enough resources to do as they would otherwise like to do, the existence of other citizens that do *not* and the persistence of various forms of domination will mean that South Africans taken together lack freedom.[57]

There have been and still are various external and internal attempts to 'escape' from this lack of freedom in South Africa. As regards external escape, it is a well-known fact that many South Africans with the power and desire to do so have left South Africa to escape from the levels of crime, fear and anxiety created by the social, economic and political ills described above. Many have also left for reasons of outright racism, a deep-rooted prejudice that must be overcome. Many of those who have left might have found greater freedom elsewhere, but there is little doubt that their individual 'escape' will not do much to change the lack of freedom that exists within South Africa, unless of course their 'escape'

---

[57] *Cf.* G. A. Cohen, 'Capitalism, Freedom and the Proletariat' in *The Liberty Reader*, ed. D. Miller (Edinburgh: Edinburgh University Press, 2006); and on 'collective unfreedom' for a similar if different analytical framework for understanding this, see L. Hamilton, 'Collective Unfreedom in South Africa', *Contemporary Politics*, 17.4 (2011), pp. 355–372; and for a critique thereof, see L. Hamilton, *Freedom is Power: Liberty Through Political* Representation (Cambridge: Cambridge University Press, 2014).

has meant an overall reduction in the amount of racism left in South Africa, which would undoubtedly make South Africans freer. In any case, those that have 'escaped' have not displayed much solidarity for the cause of the new South Africa and those that are left behind are in South Africa either out of lack of power, resources, desire (or some combination of all three) to leave, diffidence about their chances of leaving or finding more freedom elsewhere, or as a consequence of solidarity for the 'new' South Africa. In any case, the status of those that have left is of no consequence because, if they have taken up citizenship elsewhere, they are no longer South African, or at least not uniquely so; their degree of freedom is now determined by the material conditions of their new place of abode and the individual and group powers and freedoms that prevail there.

As regards the possibility for internal escape, given the foregoing account of the various dimensions of freedom and the extant forms of domination in South Africa, it seems reasonable to conclude that South Africans collectively lack freedom to significant degrees because the four forms of domination discussed above mean that the cycle of poverty for some quickly translates into a cycle of less and less freedom for all; or, in other words, humans living under collective conditions are free only if other members of the collective are also free because if any of them lack freedom as power they tend to create a similar lack of freedom in others. This is the case because their lack of power may force them to act in ways that impair the freedom of those who would otherwise have sufficient power and freedom. This is when reality bites and it comes in the form of powerlessness, violence, crime, fear and anxiety, all the result of living in a highly unequal society.

This is also where the case of South Africa highlights the stark inadequacies of the orthodox liberal account of freedom as equivalent to being 'free from interference' or 'free from politics'. To assume that you are free because you can 'do what you want' in your 'private sphere', secure behind high walls, security fencing and protected by private police forces and with sufficient resources to meet all your needs and wants is to misunderstand gravely the nature of freedom. Thus the Freedom Charter of 1955 is eerily prophetic (and very far from being realized) when it proclaims in its penultimate section entitled 'There Shall be Houses, Security and Comfort' that 'Fenced locations and ghettoes shall be abolished', although of course those that composed these lines had in mind those without adequate housing. It is a great irony of history that now the seemingly secure and comfortable have fenced themselves in to the extent that they could be said to have ghettoized themselves.

Even for the most 'secure' reality bites in the form of crime, either over the high walls or outside of the 'private sphere'. To live in a society in which large swathes of the population do not have the power to exercise, critique and generate their formal freedoms, where a smaller but economically more powerful proportion of the population either completely miscomprehends freedom or is too 'corrupted' (in Machiavelli's sense of the term) to identify it, is to live in a society and polity that collectively lacks freedom to significant degrees. It is in this sense that Mandela is right regarding freedom's indivisibility, even if he may not have articulated it in these terms. The political struggle against apartheid brought things into stark relief, but, unfortunately, so does contemporary South Africa. Freedom's indivisibility is made only more apparent, if more complex, when we conceive of it not just in terms of individual and group power, but also in terms of the freedoms and power of the political representatives of the individuals and groups that constitute South Africa, as will become evident in the next chapter.

3

Political Representation

The dawn of democracy in South Africa has fulfilled its promise to produce a consolidated representative democracy, or at least so it seems to some: although many years of 'jobless growth' have left early promises unfulfilled, the dark early morning clouds of violent upheaval, division and enmity have been replaced by the bright signs of reconciliation, periodic free and fair elections and a shared vision of the future. This spirit of reconciliation and cooperation are the results not only of the much-lauded Truth and Reconciliation Commission. It is also a direct consequence of a negotiated settlement between old and new political and economic elites, which created new forms of commercial and political representation that ensured against economic stagnation and political turmoil. But does a seemingly successful transition to democracy translate into the survival of representative democracy in the medium and long terms? Do existing forms of political representation in South Africa constitute consolidated representative democracy? More to the point, may the answer to the conundrum of two decades of mostly failed promises as regards macroeconomic management and government responsiveness to the needs of the citizenry have its source in South Africa's macro-political forms of representation?

In this chapter I argue that they do. In doing so, I suggest the South African case complicates much of the received opinion regarding the consolidation of representative democracy. Unreconstructed realists abound in these arguments, for obvious reasons: they see themselves, quite rightly, as countering the exaggerated claims of democracy's cheerleaders, who claim victory after victory as more and more countries are added to the list of new democracies (between 1980 and 2002, 81 countries moved from authoritarianism to democracy[1]); however, they also tend to give off a stench of exclusivity regarding the 'democratic club' –

---

[1] United Nations, *Human Development Report 2002: Deepening Democracy in a Fragmented World* (Oxford: Oxford University Press, 2002), cited in I. Shapiro, *The State of Democratic Theory* (Princeton: Princeton University Press, 2003), p. 2.

they suggest implicitly that by making entrance requirements to its membership sufficiently stringent, it is less likely to lose its glow of 'western civilization'. Yet their cautionary tales are felicitous in many ways. Take but two examples. At one extreme, following on from the work of Joseph Schumpeter and Samuel Huntington, it has become conventional amongst political scientists of a certain stripe to withhold judgement that a democracy has been consolidated until the governing party has twice lost an election and peacefully handed over power.[2] However, by that stringent test the United States of America was not a democracy until 1840, Japan and India have not been democracies until very recently and the jury is still out on the many democratizing countries in Latin America and the former communist world.[3] At another extreme, in which representative democracy is taken to be more a system of representative government than a form of democracy, other related and still quite stringent characteristics are proposed. These include the following: those who govern are appointed by election at regular intervals; the decision-making of the representatives is independent of the wishes of the electorate; those who are governed may give free expression of their opinions without fear of sanction from those who govern; and public decisions undergo trial of debate.[4] Although this latter set of characteristics is more accommodating, I want to suggest here that the really important answer to the question regarding whether or not a democracy has been consolidated is not so much provided by whether or not elites can compete without recourse to violence or whether or not elected representatives can act independently under the clear, critical and unrepressed view of the citizenry – even if these may also all be important – but, rather, that the healthy functioning and likely survival of a representative democracy have to do with the nature of the institutions of political representation that obtain therein and the extent to which they minimize domination and thereby constrain or enable freedom as power amongst the citizenry.

My focus here is on South Africa, but in order to determine whether its new representative democracy is healthy, empowering and likely to survive, in this chapter I elucidate first the notion of representation in relation to groups, classes, individuals and freedom as power. I then move on to the South African situation

---

[2] J. Schumpeter, *Capitalism, Socialism, and Democracy* (New York: Harper, 1942); S. Huntington, *The Third Wave: Democratization in the Late Twentieth Century* (Norman: University of Oklahoma Press, 1991). For one particularly illuminating critique of these arguments, see Shapiro, *Democratic Theory*, pp. 80ff.

[3] I. Shapiro and K. Tebeau, *After Apartheid: Reinventing South Africa* (Charlottesville: University of Virginia Press, 2011), p. 4.

[4] B. Manin, *The Principles of Representative Government* (Cambridge: Cambridge University Press, 1997), pp. 3, 6.

proper and argue that, in the light of my foregoing analysis of what forms of representation are necessary for real freedom, there are two glaring 'gaps' and associated persistent forms of domination that the existing South African system of political representation falls short on. In the first case, it tends to close a gap that ought to be kept open; in the second case, it is widening a gap it should be closing. First, South Africa's political representatives too readily succumb to the authoritarian temptation to close the gap between themselves and 'the people', or at least their representation thereof: they associate 'the party' with 'the people' and thus 'the state'. Second, South Africa's macro-political system has created *too much of a gap* between political representatives and citizens, especially regarding how the latter are able to articulate their needs and whether and how the government responds to and evaluates these needs. As I argue, the first of these is potentially related to an ill-conceived response to the second of these, but it is also to do with the ANC's history as a liberation movement and is undoubtedly a consequence of the electoral system chosen by the two groups of elites involved in debilitating and self-seeking compromises during the transition to democracy. In other words, in contrast to the more formal accounts of the consolidation of democracy summarized above – there are others too, but they would delay us – the fact that South Africa is struggling to consolidate democracy is not *explained* by reference to these formal tests, but in terms of the nature of the institutions of political representation and associated persistent forms of domination that were generated through its negotiated settlement (or elite compromise). Existing forms of representation in South Africa not only fail to enable citizens to overcome various forms of domination. They also generate an environment that is conducive to numerous practices that are deleterious to overcoming domination and generating liberty through political representation, practices such as pervasive rent-seeking, one-party dominance, corruption and impunity amongst representatives, centralized executive power and a dangerous overemphasis on unity and solidarity. The flipside of this, I argue, is another set of deleterious practices for freedom as power, however liberating they may feel in practice: a *marxisant*-inflected emphasis on active political participation. In its best form, this rests on unrealistic expectations of levels of virtue, duty and political obligation in an otherwise depoliticized population. In its most dangerous form, it fuels the frustration of the unemployed, working class and poorly serviced majority to the point of troubling and counterproductive levels of violence and destruction. While the latter response is understandable, especially given current social and economic conditions in South Africa, it is hardly a recipe for freedom.

The chapter ends by explaining how South Africa could have got itself into this predicament. The answer, I argue, lies in the nature of the elite compromise determined during the transition to democracy. The moral then is that elite compromises of the kind experienced in South Africa may enable a relatively peaceful transition to democracy, but their unique focus on existing elite interests sacrifices future freedom and stability at the altar of short-term strategy and security. The South African case, then, belies the arguments in support of a consociational arrangement, in which power elites in sharply divided societies secure transitions to democracy best by means of a political power-sharing deal.[5] There is little doubt that this is ultimately what occurred and that it has been to the great detriment of real power and freedom for most South Africans.

Representative government

What we now call representative democracy has its origins in ideas and institutions that developed in the wake of the English, American and French revolutions, more often than not in direct opposition to democracy or government by the people. For example, James Madison, in America, and Emmanuel Siéyès, in France, argued in a similar vein that representation was not an approximation of government by the people made necessary by the size and complexity of large modern states; rather, it was an essentially different and superior system particularly appropriate for modern commercial societies in which individuals were chiefly occupied in economic production and exchange.[6] Both stressed the 'huge difference' between democracy, in which citizens make the laws themselves, and the representative system of government, in which they entrust the exercise of their power, in particular their legislative or law-making power, to elected representatives.[7] Also the kind of constitution that Siéyès thought suitable for a free state was quite similar to the kind of 'not-quite republican, but not-quite royal constitution' that the Federalists advocated for the United States of America.[8]

---

[5]   R. de Kadt and C. Simkins, 'The Political Economy of Pervasive Rent-seeking', in *Thesis Eleven*, 115 (April 2013), pp. 112–126; Shapiro, *Democratic Theory*, pp. 78–103; A. Lijphart, *The Politics of Accommodation: Pluralism and Democracy in the Netherlands* (Berkeley: University of California Press, 1975); A. Lijphart, *Democracy in Plural Societies: A Comparative Exploration* (New Haven: Yale University Press, 1977).

[6]   J. Madison, 'Federalist 10' in A. Hamilton, J. Madison and J. Jay, *The Federalist*, ed. T. Ball (Cambridge: Cambridge University Press, 2003 [1787]); E. J. Sieyès, *Political Writings*, ed. M. Sonenscher (Indianapolis/Cambridge: Hackett, 2003 [1787]), p. xv; Manin, *Representative Government*, p. 2.

[7]   Sieyès, *Political Writings*; Manin, *The Principles of Representative Government*, p. 3, fn 3.

[8]   M. Sonenscher, 'Introduction', in Sieyès, *Political Writings*, p. xv.

Representative democracy has certainly seen changes over the past 200 years, for example, the extension of voting rights and the establishment of universal suffrage.[9] Certain central elements, however, have not been affected by these developments. These include the following: those who govern are appointed by election at regular intervals; the decision-making of the representatives is independent of the wishes of the electorate; those who are governed may give free expression of their opinions without fear of sanction from those who govern; and public decisions undergo trial of debate.[10]

However, Siéyès' theory of representation in particular went more emphatically beyond established usage by referring to something systematic in any durable and extensive modern human association: the division of labour and its link to increased specialization and representation. He made a distinction between two kinds of representation in modern commercial societies that both belonged to a single system. One kind of representation was to be found in all the non-political activities of everyday life. For example, he argued that the person who makes my shoes is my representative. He is representing me in utilizing a capacity common to both of us to carry out a vital function (or means) to satisfy a need of mine. Moreover, in utilizing a representative for my capacity to make my own shoes, I am reducing the amount of effort involved in meeting my need to protect my feet and thus freeing myself up to undertake other activities. Siéyès thought that this division of labour and associated plurality of representation would increase the enjoyment of people's lives and was a necessary component for the development of the arts and the sciences and thus all durable human association.[11]

The other kind of representation was the kind to be found in political society – my member of parliament is my representative, or so we assume (but see below). If either of these two replaced the other, Siéyès argued, the representative system would collapse. Although both kinds of representation have their origins in the means individuals marshall to meet their needs, they are, according to Siéyès, also fundamentally different: the kind of representation found in daily life is essentially plural whereas that of political life, essentially singular. The former was associated with the means individuals use to meet their individual needs. The latter was made up of the means individuals use to meet their common needs. Here, and in subsequent chapters, I adopt this distinction directly: by

[9] P. Rosanvallon, *Le Sacre du citoyen: Histoire du suffrage universel en France* (Paris: Gallimard, 1992); G. Eley, *Forging Democracy: The History of the Left in Europe, 1850–2000* (Oxford: Oxford University Press, 2002).

[10] Manin, *Representative Government*, pp. 3, 6.

[11] Sonenscher, 'Introduction', in Sieyès, *Political Writings*, p. xv.

'informal', 'economic' or 'commercial' representation I mean what Siéyès means by 'commercial representation', and by 'formal' or 'political' representation I mean what he meant by 'political representation', in this case representation within the political structures of South Africa's representative democracy, in particular parliament; I also show how both kinds of representation can take the form of principal–agent representation, representation as trusteeship, representation as identification or aesthetic representation, or any combination of all four, as discussed below and in greater detail in my book *Freedom is Power*.[12]

However, given my argument in the first chapter regarding needs and interests and their necessarily partisan nature, although I will make reference to common needs of a kind, and do not of course deny that their exist a few common needs of the citizenry (and of the state) as a whole, when I do infrequently refer to common needs, I will mean the partisan needs felt by subsections or subgroups of the polity in question (in this case South Africa).[13] Siéyès, likes Hobbes before him, overemphasized common needs, interests or natural rights in a more general quest for unity and singularity of the sovereign for very understandable reasons: both lived within highly divided polities where war was either ever-present or a constant threat and both pointed out, quite correctly, that besides representing individuals and groups in different sorts of ways, political representatives also represent the state. States, like other forms of association, depend upon representation in order to function at all, but to function as states they depend upon a wider claim to legitimacy than other kinds of association: a distinctive claim to represent all their citizens. Although the history of representation shows that there is nothing inherently democratic about the idea of representation, in our democratic age, we assume that to be legitimate, political representation must be democratic.

And yet these older, pre-democratic ideas regarding representation remain helpful in clarifying some incorrect assumptions regarding representative government in our democratic age. The conception of political representation that emerges from these insights is in strong contrast to the common assumption made today that political representatives represent the individual interests of particular citizens. The question of whether they do or not, most commentators assume, depends on a choice between representatives doing what their constituents want and doing what they, the representatives, think is

---

[12] L. Hamilton, *Freedom is Power: Liberty Through Political Representation* (Cambridge: Cambridge University Press, 2014), ch. 5.

[13] For more on the nature of needs, see L. Hamilton, *The Political Philosophy of Needs* (Cambridge: Cambridge University Press, 2003).

best, that is, in the 'common interest', which Hannah Pitkin calls the 'mandate-independence controversy'.[14] But this is too simplistic. As elaborated on further below, representatives could represent the interests of members of their constituency, say, without necessarily doing what the members want, and yet not have to revert to a notion of 'common interest': the representatives could do what they think is in the best interests of the members, which may *not* be what the members in fact want, and yet still successfully represent the individual interests of the members and *not* the common interest.[15] Moreover, whether or not political representatives represent individual constituency member's interests or common interests, and thus what exactly is meant by representation, depends upon a number of factors, which prove vitally important to understand the argument of this book. The history of the concept of representation is full of various conceptions of representation drawn not only from politics, but also from law, economics, literature and the theatre. These are concerned with how we represent individuals, groups, the state and, increasingly, non-governmental structures and organizations.

However, given that these pre-democratic conceptions of representation constitute a corrective to the simplistic, atomistic contemporary assumptions regarding representation, they do have some currency in contemporary thought.[16] The result is that contemporary understandings of political representation are caught between two equally problematic, related polarized positions: the representation of extreme 'diversity' – directly tracking the expressed interests of the represented (usually via some means of aggregation) – or the representation of 'unity' – the collective whole and its interests.[17] This unhelpful dichotomy is also played out within contemporary *normative* models of democracy in both their 'aggregative' and 'deliberative' forms, with both sides assuming for different reasons that all relevant interests exist antecedent to the process of

---

[14] H. F. Pitkin, *The Concept of Representation* (Berkeley, CA: University of California Press, 1967); H. F. Pitkin, 'Representation', in *Political Innovation and Conceptual Change*, ed. T. Ball, J. Farr and R. L. Hanson (Cambridge: Cambridge University Press, 1989), pp. 132–154.

[15] R. Geuss, *The Idea of a Critical Theory* (Cambridge: Cambridge University Press, 1981); Hamilton, *Needs*.

[16] D. Runciman, 'Hobbes Theory of Representation: Anti-democratic or Proto-democratic?', in *Political Representation*, ed. Shapiro et al. (Cambridge: Cambridge University Press 2009), pp. 15–34.

[17] For classic examples of the latter, see T. Hobbes, *Leviathan*, ed. R. Tuck (Cambridge: Cambridge University Press, 1996 [1651]), pp. 121, 128, 184; E. Burke, 'Speech to the Electors of Bristol', in *Selected Works of Edmund Burke* (Indianapolis, IN: Liberty Fund, 1999 [1774]), pp. 3–13; J-J. Rousseau, *Social Contract*, in J-J. Rousseau, *The Social Contract and Other Later Political Writings*, ed. V. Gourevitch (Cambridge: Cambridge University Press, 1997 [1762]), pp. 41, 58–65; Siéyès, *Political Writings*; and of the former, see R. Dahl, *Democracy and Its Critics* (New Haven: Yale University Press, 1989); A. Przeworski, S. Stokes and B. Manin, *Democracy, Accountability and Representation* (Cambridge: Cambridge University Press, 1999), p. 2.

representation itself and thus that legitimate representation must track revealed interests: the former runs scared from even a hint of paternalism, takes interests as fixed and formed and argues that the function of democratic politics is simply to find a means of aggregating avowed interests; the latter assumes the antecedent rationality of certain human interests and that reasonable deliberation under ideal, non-coercive conditions (enabling the right forms of speech act) will reveal these pre-political interests for all to agree upon.[18]

As regards individuals, there are three ways people have thought about representation that complicate the distinction between 'mandate' and 'independence': (a) as a principal–agent relation, where one person (the *principal*) appoints another (the *agent*) to perform some action or function on their behalf; (b) the idea of representatives as trustees, in which as owners of the trust for its duration, trustees act independently, but in the interest of their beneficiaries; (c) representation as identification, in which, unlike in the cases of the former two, no conscious decision to *appoint* a representative is needed, but there remains a sense in which the representative promotes my interests – this occurs when an individual identifies with the actions of another person in a way that gives that individual a stake in the other's actions.[19] Moreover, representation in politics is infrequently simply a matter of direct representation of individuals and their interests. It normally also involves groups, their interests and formal and informal representatives. This complicates political representation even further, especially given the complexity and division of labour of modern states and that our lives within and between these states are characterized by membership of a whole variety of overlapping and interdependent groups and various forms of associated representation. As will be argued, our freedom as power is therefore determined to a significant degree by a number of different variables to do with the nature, power and control of these groups and their representatives; moreover, given the nature of representation, the notion of 'control' here is complex and indirect. To understand this, it is necessary first to get to grips with the nature of groups, classes and social perspectives.

---

[18] Rousseau's argument regarding a rationally identifiable 'will of the people', 'common good' or 'general will' (see Rousseau, *Social Contract*) is the locus classicus of both traditions, the aggregative tradition exemplified by K. Arrow, *Social Choice and Individual Values* (New York: Wiley, 1951), and J. M. Buchanan and G. Tullock, *The Calculus of Consent: Logical Foundations of Constitutional Democracy* (Ann Arbor: University of Michigan Press, 1962), and the deliberative tradition, exemplified by J. Habermas, *The Theory of Communicative Action*, 2 Vols, trans. T. McCarthy (Boston: Beacon Press, 1984/7). For more on the problems of both models, see C. Hayward, 'On Representation and Democratic Legitimacy', in *Political Representation*, ed. Shapiro et al., pp. 111–135; C. Mouffe, *The Democratic Paradox* (London: Verso, 2000); and S. Wolin, 'Fugitive Democracy', in *Democracy and Difference*, ed. S. Benhabib (Princeton: Princeton University Press, 1996), pp. 31–45.
[19] M. B. Vieira and D. Runciman, *Representation* (Cambridge: Polity Press, 2008), p. 66–81.

Groups, classes and social perspectives

A group is 'a collective of individuals who are connected with each other in ways that are relevant to them, and/or others, and thereby affect their behaviour and/or that of others'.[20] The connection that binds the members of a group may be as a result of their gender, class, form of employment, lack of employment, material condition, political cause and so on. A group is therefore distinct from other kinds of associations. It is characterized by a durable connection amongst the members and one that is of significance or is meaningful. So a gathering of a collection of friends on a Sunday morning in the park is not a group in this sense, unless of course they happen to be gathering as members of, say, the Westdene – the Johannesburg suburb in which I live – Sunday morning football club, where the same (or similar) set of individuals gathers every Sunday.

Elsewhere I have compared at greater length than is possible to rehearse here the concept of 'group' and other associated concepts such as 'class' and 'social perspective'.[21] But it is probably a good idea to state unambiguously that that the notion of 'group' as articulated here does not, for a moment, assume that any single individual's identity is determined by a group identity. Individuals can and normally are 'members' of various groups within society determined by various classes, interests, perspectives and roles.[22] Individual or group identity is therefore not conceived of as essential and unchanging. Rather, resorting to the language of 'groups' is shorthand for speaking about the various groups, classes and social perspectives that exist in all modern polities. Moreover, what I say regarding groups is about the nature of groups, and not the individuals that constitute them: especially under modern conditions, individual ideals, interests and perspectives are informed and influenced by a whole range of social groups, some of which membership is not intentional – individuals often simply find themselves included within certain groups – whereas in other cases it is, that is, it involves deliberate choice. Nor does anything follow from this discussion regarding group rights: along with liberals and in opposition to communitarians, if rights turn out

---

[20] Vieira and Runciman, *Representation*, p. 86.
[21] See, in particular, Hamilton, *Freedom is Power*, ch. 5.
[22] I. Shapiro and W. Kymlicka (eds), *Ethnicity and Group Rights: NOMOS XXXIX* (New York: New York University Press, 1997); and I. Marion Young, *Inclusion and Democracy* (Oxford: Oxford University Press, 2000), esp. Chapter 4. I borrow the idea of 'social perspective' from the latter work. However, unlike Young, who develops it in response to sustained critique of her earlier emphasis on 'groups', I don't think it is fully workable; 'group', properly problematized, works better as a catch-all notion.

to be the best means of formatting politics,[23] I remain sceptical of the idea of group rights, especially regarding normative or ethical primacy. Individual rights must trump group rights because group rights can and often are used to justify traditional institutions and practices that act against the empowerment of individuals, as has been the case historically in South Africa. Also, you might very well ask, what is wrong with the notion of class? Well, not much, as will become apparent; the only problem is that it is an insufficiently broad category, for although our class perspectives and interests are of paramount importance in politics, so are other kinds of group membership and associated interests, particularly those related to gender, geography, street and satisfaction.

The individual members of groups often share similar interests, but this depends on the type and often the size of the group in question. Distinctions can be drawn between voluntary and involuntary groups, between cooperative and non-cooperative groups and between groups that have and those that do not have their own agency. Involuntary groups are normally groups into which we are born, not ones we choose or can exit at our own discretion. Voluntary groups, in contrast, are groups we join by choice and also exit freely. Then there are cooperative groups, in which the members are jointly committed to some agreed-upon goal and non-cooperative groups where this shared commitment does not exist.[24] A good example of the former is a class-based pressure group and the latter a group of actual or potential creditors. The members of the latter kind of group act of their own initiative and for their own particular goals and preferences; what makes them a group is that they may share common concerns, knowledge, interests and rules of engagement and obligation. Finally, groups can be agents and non-agents. The former have the capacity to *act* in ways that resembles individuals: they can define goals for themselves, perform tasks, appoint representatives and so on, for example, committees, governments and joint stock companies. Groups that are non-agents lack any formal organization and have no capacity to coordinate their efforts, although they share common interests. These three kinds of distinctions often cut across one another: so a group can be voluntary and cooperative and have agency, such as a labour union, and a group can be involuntary, cooperative and not have agency, such as those born into a group of unemployed, cooperative but unrepresented shack dwellers on the margins of Johannesburg, and so on and so forth.

---

[23] Something contested in R. Geuss, *History and Illusion in Politics* (Cambridge: Cambridge University Press, 2001), Hamilton, *Needs* and R. Geuss and L. Hamilton, 'Human Rights: A Very Bad Idea', *Theoria*, 60.2 (2013), pp. 83–103.

[24] Vieira and Runciman, *Representation*.

The assumption is often made that for groups to act they must have clear and explicit rules for the election or selection of representatives, which is only therefore possible for groups with agency. But this is to miss *the most important fact of the nature of many groups* and their relation to various forms of economic and political representation: groups normally acquire agency by virtue not of direct rules for the selection of representatives but of *more informal forms of representation*.

Group representation

Western political thought tends to focus on two distinct groups of people – the rulers and the ruled. The rulers are the government, sovereign powers, lawmakers or *representatives*; and the ruled are the citizens, people, voters or the *represented*. The relationship of representation holds these two groups together, and in representative democracies it enables the ruled to exercise some form of control over the rulers (at the very least via the ballot box). However, this picture is too stark: even 'the rulers' may comprise various different groups, not to mention the large diversity of groups that constitute 'the ruled'. The extent of control any subsection of the ruled has over the rulers will depend therefore upon *the relationship of representation their group or groups have with the rulers*.

As in the case of the representation of individuals, the representative of a group can be given a warrant to act on behalf of the group in various ways. First, if the group is an agent it can act as a *principal* and appoint another *agent* to perform some function on its behalf. For this to be possible, rules must exist by means of which the decisions of the group's members are put together to generate a collective decision, normally achieved though unanimity or majority decision. However, although some groups are like this, for example small-scale workers cooperatives, most groups are not as they lack the capacity for collectivized reason. Second, another possible candidate comes from the legal model of a 'trust', where property is managed by an entity (the *trustee*) for the benefit of another (the *beneficiary*) without the latter being said to own the property in question. It rests on the creation of a legal fiction: representatives or trustees act independently but in the group's name, in accordance with rules that treat the group *as if it were a principal*, and without having to be given any direct orders.[25] A third form of representation involves the identification

---

[25] F. W. Maitland, *State, Trust and Corporation*, ed. D. Runciman and M. Ryan (Cambridge: Cambridge University Press, 2003).

of interests or identities. There is no *appointment* of a representative. Rather, a representative brings forward a claim to represent a group, evidence for which is found in their capacity to attract a following, for example, NGOs acting as representatives; *or* a group can create a representative as they identify with something they do – representation by 'one of us', for example, national creditors. Members have a *presence* in the actions of the representative by dint of what the representative has in common with the group – interests, identities or values.[26]

Group representation and group freedom

As I have already stated, in western political thought political representation is normally conceived of in terms of either 'mandate' or 'independence', that is, that political representatives do or ought to respond directly to the expressed opinions and interests of the citizens they represent or, in contrast, they do or ought to act independently of these interests and judge for themselves what is in the best interests of the citizenry and state. The warrant that a representative is given is then explained by reference to a *principal–agent* relation, a relation of trusteeship or the identification of interests/identities.

In other words, all three of these accounts of representation do not escape the theoretical straightjacket of 'mandate' versus 'independence'. And this is because they all rest upon one or both of two erroneous assumptions regarding groups: (i) that the interests of group members cohere in such a way as to make them a plausible principal; and (ii) that there exist a set of shared interests or identities antecedent to and necessary for political representation. In fact, citizens' and states' needs and interests are not pre-existing and fixed, waiting to be tracked through representation. Rather, they require identification, articulation, expression, evaluation and even construction. Needs and interests are more objective than wishes, opinions and preferences. They are more easily detached from any specific group of 'holders' (e.g. the collective interest in a sustainable environment), but they are never totally unattached either. Similar to needs, interests have a dualistic nature – they are attached and unattached, subjective and objective – and this lies at the heart of the *ambiguities of any form of interest group representation*.[27] Individual and group interests become *present* as a result

---

[26] Vieira and Runciman, *Representation*, pp. 111, 103.
[27] Pitkin, *Representation*.

of representation, that is, they may only be experienced, identified and expressed as a result of the actions and concerns of representatives.

Thus, representative institutions will not be freedom-enhancing if they simply 'track' interests; rather, they must encourage the formation of new political interests, especially in conditions in which existing relations of power create or reinforce situations of domination. This is most obvious in a place like South Africa today, where many existing felt needs and interests have been formed under conditions of racist policies, extreme poverty, inequality and unemployment. Domination under these conditions could never be overcome by means of representation, simply 'tracking' articulated interests. Representatives have to generate new interests actively that enable groups to escape these situations of domination. Therefore the relationship between group representation and group freedom is one in which the freedom of the group is dependent upon whether or not the representative of the group can generate the right kinds of new interests *and* then can defend them in the relevant formal institutions of representation. It follows from all this that the individual freedom as power depends upon four associated variables: (a) the nature and relative power of the groups of which one is a member; (b) the relationship of representation that exists between the members of the group and the group's representatives; (c) the relative power of the groups' representatives; and (d) the relationship between one's groups' representatives and the formal political representatives of one's polity.

There exists, though, another more helpful alternative account of representation, an 'aesthetic' theory of political representation, that escapes these erroneous presuppositions. As we know from the world of art and literature, representation is never simply the copy of some pre-existing external reality.[28] Representation always creates something new. For example, Leo Tolstoy's account of the Napoleonic War does not simply replicate the historical events; it creates a new version of it in the act of representing it. There is therefore always a 'gap' between an object and the representation of that object and this holds in politics too: as Frank Ankersmit puts it, 'political reality is not first given to us and subsequently represented; political reality comes into being after and due to representation'.[29] Political representatives can never therefore merely speak for the interests of the people as they existed before being represented; instead the act of *representing them creates a new version of the people and their interests*, and this creative process gives representation its dynamism. Some people,

---

[28] Vieira and Runciman, *Representation*, pp. 138–139.
[29] F. Ankersmit, *Aesthetic Politics: Political Philosophy Beyond Fact and Value* (Stanford: Stanford University Press, 1997), p. 47.

such as Rousseau and certain nineteenth-century 'anarchists', interpret this negatively, in the sense that they suppose that it follows from this that political representation and freedom are antithetical.[30] What is novel about the aesthetic approach is that it highlights the positive, creative aspect of this characteristic of political representation. It provides a means of understanding that political representation is not designed as a means either to 'track' pre-existing interests or to provide an *exact* reflection of the people and their interests or identities; rather it is designed to give the people an image of themselves upon which to reflect.[31] This 'gap' between the rulers and the ruled is itself filled by groups and their representatives, and so it is in this gap that the degree of a group's freedom is played out.

But how exactly does the aesthetic theory help us grasp the way group representation is related to group freedom?

First, the aesthetic theory of representation establishes that representatives give the people an image of themselves upon which to reflect. Representation itself opens up a gap between the government and the people.[32] I add the idea that it is possible to see this best if we *analyse how this gap is filled* by various group representatives with varying relations of power between themselves and those that govern, power relations that are characterized by more or less domination and thus enable more or less freedom as power for the representatives and thereby for the groups in question.

Second, the aesthetic approach to representation highlights the important fact that needs and interests are never pre-existing and fixed in politics, as discussed earlier.

Third, in any system of representative democracy there will be more than one version of 'the people' at work. There is 'the people' conjured up by formal political representatives in the act of speaking for them; there are conflicting views of 'the people' generated by group membership and representation, what Dunn has called the 'capacity for protracted and confident self-organization of the bearers of different social interests'[33]; in addition, there are 'the people' who pass judgement on these conjuring acts. Indeed, the functioning of representative

---

[30] Rousseau, *Social Contract*; and P-J. Proudhon, *What Is Property?*, ed. D. R. Kelly and B. G. Smith (Cambridge: Cambridge University Press, 1994).

[31] Vieira and Runciman, *Representation*, p. 139; F. Ankersmit, *Political Representation* (Stanford: Stanford University Press, 2002), pp. 112ff.

[32] Ankersmit, *Aesthetic Politics*; Ankersmit, *Political Representation*; C. Lefort, *Democracy and Political Theory* (Minneapolis: University of Minnesota Press, 1988).

[33] J. Dunn, 'The Politics of Representation and Good Government in Post-colonial Africa', in *Political Domination in Africa*, ed. P. Chabal (Cambridge: Cambridge University Press, 1986), p. 147.

democracy depends upon politicians being able to offer *competing versions of the people to the people*, in order for the voters to be able to choose the one they prefer.[34] Given this, the aesthetic theory of representation allows us to view representative democracy as a form of politics that *accommodates* aspects of all three of the other models of representation, and it does so by emphasizing the central role played by political judgement amongst both the representative and the represented. If groups and their representatives are given increasingly greater parity of power and control (and thus freedom), it is possible to see how groups and their representatives can have principal–agent, trustee and identity relationships of representation: the people with an active role, as the arbiters of representation, act much like principals; the people with a passive role, as the objects of representation, act much like trusts; and in their judgement of the image offered to them by their various representatives, individual citizens often side with whom they identify or with whom they think will defend their interests. Moreover, in most instances of these three cases, their interests and thus forms of representation are partisan, not general or common.

Finally, none of the versions of the 'the people' on offer to 'the people' ought ever to succeed in *closing the gap* between the represented and their representatives. Even the attempt to close the gap between the people and their representatives is futile and dangerous: it is not the realization of democracy but an invitation to tyranny because it thwarts any opportunity for the people to reflect on and judge the decisions and actions of their representatives.[35] As Niccolo Machiavelli and James Madison have argued, this is the case because the effect of *closing the gap* – and at the extreme the complete identification of the rulers and the ruled – is (paradoxically) to *exclude* the people from politics in their active, or judgemental, role. If the gap is closed there is no longer any room for the various groups and associated partisan interests that constitute 'the people' to evaluate the images of themselves on offer. The effect of closing the gap will be to remove the possibility for the portrayal of other competing images or visions of the polity (and associated often-competing interests).

So, thus far I have argued that freedom is power in the sense that an individual's freedom depends on her power to act and the requirements for that power across four dimensions; and that, given complex modern states, that power depends on the nature and power of group representatives and the power of represented and representatives to enact critical, political judgements.

[34] Vieira and Runciman, *Representation*, p. 141.
[35] Ankersmit, *Aesthetic Politics*, pp. 51–56; and Ankersmit, *Political Representation*, pp. 112ff.

But before I continue, there is one important caveat. This is not an exhaustive account of freedom: power and control across the four dimensions I outlined in Chapter 1 are necessary (but not sufficient conditions) for freedom. Freedom as power via group representatives allows for the possibility that individual freedom may only be fully accomplished by the individual, and that may vary depending on the individual in question. Freedom for some might be about being true to oneself whatever the demands of others, for others it may be about being embedded and determined by these duties and for yet others it might even be the life of the ascetic.

Minding the gaps in South Africa

South Africans lack meaningful representation in all of the four ways just outlined. In particular, they lack the power to affect interests, policies and representatives for three main reasons. First, in South Africa the *unemployed* as a group tend not to have meaningful representation, despite dubious claims to the contrary by the ANC that they represent them and despite the fact that many vote for the ANC. And this is not only because they lack organization and representatives, but also because their situation of poverty makes their immediate interests poor competitors in the race to reflect a successful version or vision of 'the people'.

Second, the system of closed party list proportional representation used in South Africa excludes alternative versions or visions of the polity since it is based on a conception of political representation in which the legislature directly reflects the electoral tally of parties rather than either the interests of the electorate as a whole (or vision thereof) or the partisan interests of constituents and groups. This is the case due to the nature of the electoral and institutional system that, in 1993, was chosen for post-apartheid South Africa. Ostensibly, the choice was made for its simplicity, inclusiveness and fairness, with those involved in the choice arguing that by promoting broad representivity and equity it would be sensitive to the divisions in the country, the volatility of the political situation and the urgent need for reconciliation. In effect, the entire country is taken as one voting district, and the 400 members of the National Assembly are all elected by voters choosing political parties whose pre-published party lists then determine in exact proportion to their electoral success who becomes a national political representative. Moreover, the members of the other house in this bicameral system, the National Council of Provinces, are not even voted in by the general public; they are appointed by provincial legislatures to represent each province. This latter, supposedly 'upper' house has turned out to be ineffectual. In other words, for the legislature that counts, or is supposed to count (about which more is discussed later), the National assembly, not only do electors not select individual representatives but parties, but also the political representatives who are selected are not linked to or emanate from specific geographical areas (or constituencies).[36] In this sense, South Africa's electoral system is in fact very rare. Only Israel has the same system. In every other democracy in the world citizens are represented by where they live, though exactly how and what proportion of the representatives is elected in this fashion vary quite widely.[37] In South Africa, identical proportionality of party support in parliament – or a miniature, exact copy of 'the people' – sacrifices the 'gap' between the representation of the people and the people themselves, and the potential for competition amongst various visions and interests.

In recent times this has been exemplified by the ruling party as it repeatedly and aggressively claims that it alone represents 'the people'; as it erodes the power of the legislative arm of government; and as it fails to distinguish between the state and the party. Two examples of the latter stand out: (a) when the party makes a decision it claims that it is a decision made by 'the people' (as with the recall of Mbeki as president); and (b) when it is suggested that democracy in South Africa is safe since 'the party' structures are fully democratic. *These claims mistakenly identify 'the party' with 'the people' and thus 'the state',* which not only gives the party the unique and complete legitimacy of rule that it seeks, but also *silences all other* claims to represent 'the people' – a distinct stench of stalinism. This is a deeply ironic and unfortunate development since in healthy polities political parties are some of the many important groups and representatives that occupy the gap between the rulers and the ruled.[38] At present in South Africa the ruling party is usurping the power of the people as it situates itself as a microcosm or exact copy of the democratic polity it ought to be creating: the party attempts to represent the people (in the sense of being a copy of them) rather than act as one amongst many representative versions of the people and their interests for the people to judge and choose. The fact that one party is still so dominant only exacerbates this lack of freedom, as does the fact that the party rules as part of

---

[36] The Forum for Public Dialogue (FPD), 'Electoral Systems and Accountability: Comparative Case Studies and Lessons for South Africa', Working Paper Draft, 23 July 2013, pp. 46–48. The ANC does now link representatives to geographic areas, but the link is random, only determined following the election process and few if any representatives seem to take it seriously – they do not reside in or feel that it is necessary to visit the citizens who live in the areas they are supposed to represent. I am very grateful to Kathlena Walther and Roger Southall for allowing me to see and sending me a copy of this unpublished document.

[37] A. Rehfeld, *The Concept of Constituency: Political Representation, Democratic Legitimacy, and Institutional Design* (Cambridge: Cambridge University Press, 2005), p. 3.

[38] Ankersmit, *Political Representation*, pp. 125–132.

a tri-partite alliance with the South African Communist Party (SACP) and the main Trade Union umbrella body (COSATU). However, this dominance of one party does not explain many of South Africa's problems, as many commentators assume. It itself requires explanation, and part of that explanation at least can be found in the various (deleterious) effects of South Africa's electoral system combined with the fact that the head of state and the head of government – normally kept separate by the office of the constitutional monarch/president and that of the prime minister – are equivalent, in the sense that they are both held by the same person, the president. Moreover, the president is chosen by parliament and is thus normally also the majority party's president or leader. Hence, it is no wonder the necessary, firm distinctions between state, government and ruling party can become easily blurred.

Third, at least one-third of the population is either unemployed or no longer economically active (either as a consequence of illness, age and disability or because they are actively discouraged work-seekers, that is, those who are able to work but have not been able to find work for so long that they have stopped looking for work). The number of South Africa's unemployed now stands at 4.54 million, or a formal unemployment rate of 25.7%; the number of economically inactive workers stands at a staggering 14.35 million (with actively discouraged work-seekers comprising just under 2 million of this total); thus, even if we consider only the actively discouraged work-seekers and the formally unemployed, we have a *real unemployment rate of approximately 37% of the population.*[39] If this percentage is combined with that proportion of the population that is involved in menial and underpaid jobs (quintiles two and three of the 'household head income survey'), whose representatives come from trade unions *affiliated to COSATU, the union umbrella body that rules with the ANC and thus provides little critical purchase on the rulers or representatives,* and we assume that the unemployed household heads occupy the lowest quintile, on a conservative estimate we can only conclude that a staggering 77% of South Africans have little or no meaningful representation.[40] In terms of my argument here regarding

---

[39] Statistics SA's Labour Force Survey, quoted in *Business Day*, Friday 29 July 2011; the situation has worsened since the previous survey, when 4.3 million were unemployed, giving a formal unemployment rate of 25.3% – see 'Labour Force Survey 2009' in Statistics South Africa Quarterly Labour Force Survey Quarter 2, 2010, Available from: http://www.statssa.gov.za/publications/P0211/P02112ndQuarter2010.pdf. This calculation is corroborated by the latest (2011) census, which in fact puts this 'expanded' unemployment rate at a staggering 40% of the population. See Statistics South Africa, Census 2011: Statistical Release (Revised), P0301.4. Available from: http://www.statssa.gov.za/publications/P03014/P030142011.pdf [accessed 25 May 2013].

[40] There are five quintiles of household head income. The three lower quintiles include all those with an income of R30,000 ($4,000) per annum or less; 72.5% of the 'black' population, 44% of the 'coloured'

freedom and representation, this large section of South Africa's population lack freedom as a direct result of their lack of meaningful representation: *either* they have no agents, trustees, defenders of their identities/interests or varieties of possible images upon which to reflect *or* they have powerless representatives, whose powerlessness is a consequence of the persistence of domination within existing power relations or institutional arrangements that do not enable effective representation. South Africa is not unusual in Africa: according to John Dunn, this poor representation of the interests of what he calls the 'middling ranks' and the proletariat is common across Africa.[41]

The remaining 23% of South Africa's population vary in wealth and are no longer homogeneous in terms of race, but two related things can be said of them. First, they have much more meaningful representation, especially economic representation, in the form of identification with state creditors and in terms of either being or being represented by South Africa's capital-owning class, who, before and following political transition, gained assurances from the new political elite that their capital would not be threatened.[42] Second, despite this, they too lack freedom, if for slightly different reasons. In order to maintain their 'secure' existence they have to lock themselves up behind high walls and gated communities, only to find that this fails. Reality bites anyway in the form of powerlessness in the face of crime, fear and a depleted, privatized existence. They lack power for different reasons to the 77% of the population discussed earlier, but this lack of freedom as power still results from an environment of poor political representation.

One of the ruling party's *responses* to these problems regarding meaningful representation has been to focus on possible developments at the *local* government level. But this is not a response to the problem for two main reasons. First, given apartheid's obsession with separate development, locality, land and place in particular, and much of the history of colonial and post-colonial Africa in general, the emphasis on the representation of local community is often deeply retrogressive and the opposite of freedom-enhancing, as the continued political

---

population, 15% of the 'indian' population and 3% of the 'white' population (all post-apartheid government statistical agencies still use these apartheid race categorizations) are situated within these lowest three quintiles; hence, given the demographics of South Africa the lower three quintiles comprise 55% of the population earning a monetary income. The figure of 77% is reached by adding together the real proportion of the population that is unemployed (37%) and the percentage of the population that is employed but occupy quintiles two and three (40%). Statistics South Africa. 2009. *Income and Expenditure of Households 2005/2006*. Available from: http://www.statssa.gov.za/publications/P0100/P01002005.pdf.

[41] Dunn, 'Representation and Good Government in Africa', pp. 151ff.

[42] L. Hamilton and N. Viegi, 'Debt, Democracy and Representation in South Africa', *Representation*, 45.2 (2009), pp. 193–212.

power of non-elected chiefs in South Africa's rural areas and the associated
poor representation of women's interests exemplifies well.[43] Second, the various
attempts to enhance democratic participation of the citizenry at the local level
is misplaced as it is based on the premise that the problem regarding national
representative politics arises as a consequence of lack of citizen participation.
However, as I have argued, *the problem is not about the degree or form of citizens'*
political participation but about the way in which representation is being enacted
in South Africa. Moreover, even if we were to assume for argument's sake that
the logic behind these initiatives is a good one, it amounts to nothing more than
window-dressing. Although citizens are given some access to deliberation prior
to decision-making, it is ward councillors who ultimately make the decisions
behind closed doors and most have firm party loyalty, not least of all because,
in accordance with the electoral system specified in the constitution, half of
the councillors are instated through proportional representation, whilst the
remaining half are ward constituent representatives. Therefore, as is the case
at the national level, *councillors are not accountable to their constituencies*
but accountable to party leaders.[44] The other problem is, of course, that ward
councillors have very little power. Most of the more important decisions
regarding policy and resource allocation occur at the provincial and national
levels, and increasingly – due again to the structural power inadvertently handed
to the ruling party – at the level of the national executive (and thus the ANC as
majority party) as opposed to the legislature, the legitimate forum and source for
these deliberations and decisions.

This localized attempt at greater participation is, as introduced earlier, the
other, related way in which the poor regulation of the requisite gap between
citizens and representatives is being maintained in South Africa. In this case, it
is not that the gap is being closed too vigorously, but rather that the gap between
representative and citizen is too wide. As elaborated on above, the effect of
identical proportionality of party support in parliament or a miniature, exact
copy of 'the people' sacrifices the 'gap' between the representation of the people
and the people themselves, and the potential for competition amongst various
visions and interests. For the effect of greatest consequence of the choice of this

---

[43] *Cf.* Shapiro, *Democratic Theory*, p. 102; Dunn, 'Representation and Good Government in Africa',
pp. 152–153.

[44] C. Tapscott, 'The Challenges of Building Participatory Government', in *Participatory Governance:*
Citizens and the State in South Africa, ed. Thompson (African Centre for Citizenship and
Democracy: University of the Western Cape 2007), p. 87, Available from: http://www.accede.
co.za/downloads/monograph.pdf [accessed 15 August 2010]; L. Piper, K. Barichievy and B. Parker,
'Assessing "participatory governance" in Local Government: A Case-study of Two South African
Cities', *Politeia*, 24.3 (2005), pp. 370–393.

form of electoral system is the decoupling of parties from class or group bases. The kind of electoral system that currently prevails in South Africa in effect provides impetus for all parties to be as catch-all as possible, and thus it is no surprise that the largest, predominant and now most catch-all party was once the alliance that spearheaded the liberation from apartheid. Ironically, this has meant not just a decoupling of parties from classes, but a decoupling of this ruling alliance from the people they are supposed to represent: this second sense, where what has followed, is too much of a gap between the people and the ANC-headed ruling alliance. The combination of supposedly meaningful local participation within local, municipal structures with little power and the complete dislocation of national representatives from the people has generated a very dangerous blend of citizen frustration and poor accountability regarding the country's elected national representatives. The only individuals to whom local residents can realistically appeal in order to have their vital needs satisfied do not have the means to generate much change of policy or direction of funds, nor do they have the will as their jobs depend more on pleasing their party masters than the public they are supposed to serve. The result has been a sharp increase of violent unrest often directed at local councillors, many of whom face the very real prospect of death or serious harm as their offices and homes are razed to the ground. At the same time the country's elected national representatives can 'linger in indecision, laze in complacency and deliver poor (or no) service while local communities have no visible culprit at whom to point a finger'.[45]

National representatives are not held accountable because the gap between them and the people is so wide and well guarded by party interests that many feel a kind of impunity regarding their every action or lack of action. This is the case because the electoral system ensures against any quick change in ruling party or support thereof, as does the very inefficient and meagre forms of social welfare provided by the ANC-led governing alliance. A closed party list PR system may ensure exact proportionality of representation in parliament, but it does so by sacrificing the accountability that is necessary to keep the government working for the people. If there is no real prospect of losing the next election, due in part to a population socialized by the history of apartheid into accepting powerlessness and now further placated by social grants, there is no incentive either to be more efficient in the provision of public services or put in place macroeconomic policy that enables growth and employment or, most importantly, change the macro-political structure of election and legislation adopted in 1993. Moreover,

---

[45] FPD, 'Electoral Systems and Accountability', p. 50.

this kind of political structure lends itself not only to patrimonial politics – keeping resources and power within the ruling party – but also to rent-seeking by both economic and political elites. Once you have the right, basic training and party contacts, it becomes relatively easy to seek out and charge very high rents. The new 'black' and 'white' economic and political elite have been quick to pick up on this, and it is no wonder that the same faces and names keep cropping up, for after having spent six months in one managerial position they can charge an even higher rent and move to another. This merry-go-round of rent-seeking may be good for the pockets of a few, but it is very bad for the efficient running of South Africa's large quasi-public parastatal corporations and private corporations, many of which directly serve the poor and unemployed. In other words, one of the main sources of the lack of freedom as power of the majority of the population is the near-complete irrelevance of accountability for the 'functioning' of the macro-political structure and associated forms of debilitating rent-seeking that ensues.[46]

This condition of little or no meaningful representation and little or no elite accountability, that is, simultaneously and ironically too little and too much of a gap between the people and their representatives, is unhealthy for any state, let alone a new, emerging democracy and it does not bode well for the future. The exact causes of the poor health of South Africa's polity and economy may not be plain for all to see, but what is currently unambiguously clear is that large cracks are beginning to appear in the ruling alliance's representation of 'the people'. From well before the FIFA Football World Cup in 2010, the country has been wracked by prolonged strikes and service delivery protests, only the most infamous of which was widely reported, the Marikana massacre of 34 miners during an unprotected strike at the Lonmin Platinum mine in the North West Province. Matters were coming to a head even prior to Marikana: in 2012 alone there were more than 400 community demonstrations and protests, popularly termed 'service delivery protests', easily the highest per annum since 2004, and 88% of them were violent.[47] The lucky few who are employed and can pay to have their vital needs met or those who are able to meet some of their vital needs via government provision of free services and social grants of various sorts are often willing and able to contest the image that the ruling alliance has tried to conjure up of them, but due to existing forms of political representation

---

[46] I owe a special debt to Nicola Viegi for insightful comments on rent-seeking and poor public service; see also De Kadt and Simkins 'The Political Economy of Pervasive Rent-seeking'.

[47] FPD, 'Electoral Systems and Accountability'; and Research by Municipal IQ, cited in 'Police Not Backing Down on Violent Protests, says Minister', *Business Day*, 9 August 2012.

they lack the real freedom to contest this image by means of legal, non-violent channels. Outrage over years of jobless growth and very poor 'service delivery' driven by corruption and incompetence is manifest and there is evidence that the three parts of the ruling alliance no longer portray the same unified image. The possible outcomes are revolution or a successful decoupling of the alliance and the institution of effective and meaningful representation for all groups.[48]

In other words, there is now real and serious evidence that the inadequate macro-political forms of representation and selection of elite rulers and its concomitant effects, such as rent-seeking, one-party (ANC alliance) dominance, an oft-rolled-out and ideologically distorted discourse of unity and social solidarity generate not only various deleterious indirect costs on freedom as power, but also actual or threatened weekly violent strikes. That very real frustrations and inequalities are becoming manifest as very real and dangerous violent expressions of extreme discontent is understandable, given the social and economic conditions of much of South Africa's population. However, that it is being expressed and legitimized by activists and civil society leaders in terms of a warped, *marxisant* account of political participation is troubling, not least of all because it is a prime example of illusion and false hope in politics. As I argued in the first chapter, especially if conceived of in terms of defending human rights, it acts as the modern version of Marx's notion of religion as the opiate of the people. It does so because it not only is unsuccessful in its goals and engenders worse forms of authoritarian reactions from the government, but also gives citizens with no real institutional means to express and demand their needs a *feeling* or *sense* that they do have means of doing so, even if it is 'on the street', via illegal and violent means. Moreover, it depends upon and is articulated in terms of unrealistic expectations of citizen virtue, duty and political obligation from an otherwise depoliticized and powerless citizenry. To espouse the idea that these methods will generate anything like freedom as power – or even rectify the parlous state of delivery of economic and political goods to a previously disadvantaged majority – is to be guilty of naïvete, at best, and the purveyance of false hope, at worst.

There are two reasons for this. First, to try and paper over the problem regarding the consequences of South Africa's distorted representation by supposedly bolstering local participation and civil society is, as I've argued, disingenuous, not least of all as direct political activism ultimately takes the form of 'private' legal action against the government focused on particular parts

---

[48] *Cf.* A. Mngxitama, 'Tripartite Tussle? Get Real, It's Just a Game', *Mail & Guardian*, 3–9 September 2010.

of existing law that is in conflict with constitutional law. It does not enhance political agency, power and thus freedom.[49] The combination of 'private' activism and unelected court officials can significantly skew the agenda under conditions of little or no representative accountability combined with the supremacy of the constitution and its articulation in terms of human rights, about which more is discussed later. Owing to the lack of political agency created by macro-political institutions of representation, citizens have little other avenues but to enact their agency, especially when criticizing existing policy or law either by hyper-legal and atomistic rights-based means or by means of extra-legal and often violent expression of frustration on the streets. Little then has changed for South Africa, especially regarding the poor and poorly represented taking to the streets in an attempt to expel frustrations and express their needs – for they have no other means to do so. As the very unsuccessful programme of land reform since 1995 in South Africa attests well, human rights-based litigation, in the main, remains the preserve of those with the financial means to access the law courts, exceptions such as the Treatment Action Campaign for adequate roll-out of antiretroviral treatment for HIV/AIDS notwithstanding.[50]

Human rights activism, civic duty and consensus

This lack of political power and thus freedom via meaningful political representation has deep roots in South Africa's apartheid past, despite the seemingly novel institutional departures framing contemporary South Africa's politics. The tragic irony is that the attainment of freedom articulated in terms of human rights is partly the result of three highly significant moments in the struggle against apartheid, including two apartheid massacres. The first is the Freedom Charter, which was formally adopted on 26 June 1955 at a Congress of the People in Kliptown, the oldest residential district of Soweto, Johannesburg. It is the statement of core principles of the South African Congress Alliance, which consisted of the ANC and its allies in the South African Indian Congress, the South African Congress of Democrats and the Coloured People's Congress.[51] The significance of the charter is manifold. First, it is one of the first formal

---

[49] Cf. A. Barry, 'The Moral Psychology of Human Rights in South Africa', unpublished MA thesis, University of Johanessburg.
[50] Hamilton, *Needs*; L. Hamilton, 'Human Needs, Land Reform and the South African Constitution', *Politikon*, 33.2 (2006), pp. 133–145; cf. Barry, 'Human Rights'.
[51] ANC, 'The Freedom Charter' (2011 [1955]), Available from: http://www.anc.org.za/show.php?id=72 [accessed 30 July 2013].

documents produced by the ANC following its first serious strides in becoming a mass, non-racial movement, following the adoption in 1949 of a Programme of Action and the Defiance Campaign of 1952–1953, where unjust laws were breached by protests that courted arrest.[52] In a short space of time Congress membership soared from less than 5,000–100,000.[53] Second, it was the result of widespread consultation. The ANC sent out 50,000 volunteers countrywide to collect 'freedom demands' from the people of South Africa.[54] Third, the Charter has been of great historical significance for the ANC and its partners in the Alliance. It became the basic vision of the ANC and has remained so to this day: by 1958 all provincial congresses of the ANC had adopted the Freedom Charter as had all of its partners, it was re-emphasized in 1994 and was highlighted as a goal of the 2007 52nd ANC National Conference in Polokwane by both the Deputy Minister of Finance, Jabu Moleketi, and Head of Policy in the Presidency, Joel Netshitenze.[55] Unfortunately, you would be hard pressed to find the realization of any of its substantive demands in South Africa today. Some of its claims for formal equality and rights have been successfully institutionalized; but, as Chapter 2 showed in detail, opportunity for all does not exist, the doors of learning are not open for all, poverty, inequality and unemployment statistics have hardly changed (and in some cases have worsened) since the end of apartheid; illiteracy is still extant; land reform is stalled; free, adequate medical care is a distant dream; fenced locations and ghettoes abound and grow by the day; racism is rife and the heralded reconciliation of the Truth and Reconciliation Commission has given way to the harsh realities of a still deeply divided society.

The two apartheid massacres were those at Sharpeville on 21 March 1960, approximately 30 kilometres south of Kliptown, and at Soweto on 16 June 1976. Both have similarly reverberated through South Africa's subsequent history. At Sharpeville, a crowd of about 5,000 protesters (the police supposedly believed they were confronted by a crowd of 20,000), led by the Pan-Africanist Congress (PAC), assembled peacefully and amiably before the police station to protest against the pass laws and pass books that 'blacks' were forced to carry on their person at all times. There, completely unprovoked, 168 police officers armed with .303 rifles, Sten guns and heavy machine guns opened fire, discharging

---

[52] W. Beinart, *Twentieth-Century South Africa* (Oxford: Oxford University Press, 2001), p.154; B. Turok, *From the Freedom Charter to Polokwane: The Evolution of ANC Economic Policy* (Cape Town: New Agenda, 2008), p. 35; T. Karis, and G. M. Carter, *From Protest to Challenge: A Documentary History of African Politics in South Africa, 1882–1964, Vol 2* (Stanford: Hoover Institution Press, 1973), p. 337.

[53] T. Lodge, *Politics in South Africa: from Mandela to Mbeki* (Cape Town: David Philip, 2002), p. 34.

[54] ANC, 'The Freedom Charter'.

[55] Turok, *Freedom Charter*, p. 23.

1,344 rounds of ammunition (some explosive 'dum-dum' rounds) into the crowd, killing 69 people (including women and children) and wounding at least three times this number, many of whom were shot in the back as they ran away from volley after volley of gunfire.[56] During the Soweto student uprising, between 10,000 and 20,000 high school students protested in the streets of Soweto in response to the introduction of Afrikaans as a medium of instruction in schools, against whom the police opened fire, killing at least 176 people (some estimates suggest a figure as high as 700).

These two massacres have been very significant for South Africa's subsequent history for seven main reasons. First, they showed beyond doubt to South Africans and to the world the lengths the apartheid regime would go to, to crush mercilessly any protests against it. And yet, second, the massacre and its associated happenings 'certainly constituted a political crisis, creating an atmosphere in which serious weaknesses in the state's authority could become apparent even to senior officials and amongst privileged citizens'.[57] Third, they portrayed graphically the level of mass support that existed for those involved in trying to liberate South Africa. Fourth, thus they spurred on an entire echelon of 'black' political leadership to commit itself to doctrines of revolutionary political change. Fifth, they left those who were willing to absorb realistically what they had heard and seen in no doubt of the extent to which apartheid South Africa disempowered, disenfranchised, impoverished, oppressed and dominated most of its own population. Sixth, they drew the world's attention to the anti-apartheid struggle in ways that the ANC alone could never do: 'after 1960 "anti-apartheid" became a global preoccupation ... international anti-apartheid campaigning is acknowledged to have built "one of the most influential post-war social movements"'.[58] Finally, they showed, if in different ways, that the power and desire to confront the apartheid state was by no means the sole property or concern of the ANC and its leadership.

Importantly, as Lodge argues convincingly, despite the fact that the South African police had, on many occasions prior to Sharpeville, opened fire on protesters, and on one occasion killed many more (the Bulhoek massacre on 24 May 1921 when 183 members of the millenarian Israelite sect were killed by 800 police), and the fact that the colonial history of the continent as a whole is filled with massacres of this sort, something different happened at and following

[56] T. Lodge, *Sharpeville: An Apartheid Massacre and Its Consequences* (Oxford: Oxford University Press, 2011), pp. 10–23; 94–108.

[57] Lodge, *Sharpeville*, p. 23.

[58] Lodge, *Sharpeville*, p. 234, citing H., Thorn, *Anti-Apartheid and the Emergence of a Global Civil Society* (Basingstoke: Palgrave Macmillan, 2009), p. 5.

Sharpeville. It elicited compassion and empathy worldwide on a scale not conceivable until that time, 'feelings that helped mobilize a powerful movement of international solidarity, a movement that had it not been for the massacre may well have remained a limited concern of informed minorities and special interests'. This internationalized the anti-apartheid cause, which was a major factor in helping to 'ensure that South Africa's political transition was through a relatively orderly process of negotiation'.[59] The sheer brutality of the massacres coupled with international cultural and political shifts generated a level of empathy with 'black' South Africans in Europe and North America on a scale that had not been seen before. Moreover, and most importantly not only for the ultimate success of the liberation struggle but also for the important role played by international activists, this empathy and solidarity was articulated expressly and repeatedly in the language of human rights. In fact, besides becoming one of the most influential post-war social movements, the struggle against apartheid in South Africa also became the standard-bearer of the new language of human rights.[60]

This might have been a good thing for the struggle itself, but once liberation was achieved it has become an ideological cloak for a skewed and corrupt political order that has not generated real freedom as power and under current conditions of representation cannot generate real freedom as power. Those who claim that the current ANC-led political order has failed South Africans as it fails to live up to the founding principles of the Charter or that it pours scorn on those who lost their lives at Sharpeville or Soweto and beyond are right in one sense and wide off the mark in another. They are right in the sense that many of the leaders of the ANC today are corrupt and inept. But they are wrong to assume that the models of how best to achieve real freedom under conditions of formal political liberty can take anything from the language, models and precedents of the actions of those who fought the oppressive apartheid regime. The Freedom Charter, for example, is essentially a cry for political freedom: liberation from alien/colonial/apartheid rule; specified freedoms and rights for all, in particular rights to association, freedom of speech and electoral participation; and the institutional requirements for all to live a meaningful life. It is, in essence, an appeal to overthrow the unjust and tyrannical regime of apartheid. Moreover, being a document of its time, the Charter's emphasis on rights is a direct consequence of the global currency of these notions at the time, thanks, in part, to the adoption by the United Nations (UN) General Assembly on 10 December

---

[59] Lodge, *Sharpeville*, p. 23.
[60] L. Hunt, *Inventing Human Rights: A History* (New York: Norton, 2008); Lodge, *Sharpeville*.

1948 of the Universal Declaration of Human Rights. In any case, besides some revolutionary flourishes, again a consequence of context – the fact that it is the foundational document for the ANC's drive to become a mass movement in opposition to apartheid – its central claims, such as '[a]ll people shall have the right to live where they please, be decently housed, and to bring up their families in comfort and security' and '[t]he law shall guarantee to all their right to speak, to organize, to meet together, to publish, to preach, to worship and to educate their children', are reminiscent of a whole range of liberal thinkers from Locke[61] to J. S. Mill[62] and Rawls.[63] The Freedom Charter is therefore hardly a revolutionary document in the socialist or communist sense of that term or in the sense that is needed today in South Africa – to revolutionize existing forms of political representation to generate real freedom for all. Those who hold it up as policy panacea for all of South Africa's current political, economic and social problems are abusing the significance and function of this historical document.

In other words, to interpret such a Charter as a set of policy directives set in stone for continued populist uprising in terms of continued struggle for human rights is to undermine both the letter and the point of the document. It is a set of broad means and goals for the power necessary for all South African citizens to overcome political tyranny and a rallying cry for a movement attempting to become properly a mass movement to disrupt the normal, orderly functioning of an oppressive state. The means are constant insurrection; the goal human rights for all. Thus, my use of the idea that the 'revolution is still pending' is not intended to suggest that the revolution of the future is a good idea; rather, it is intended as a warning to all South Africans that without serious non-revolutionary changes to our economy and polity, real, uncontrolled and potentially self-defeating populist revolution is feasibly around the corner. Ironically, the constant recourse to the Freedom Charter, to Sharpeville and to Soweto as historical exemplars of how best to fight for human rights and thereby gain real freedom undermines the possibility of attaining the forms of political representation under conditions of formal political liberty that are necessary for real political freedom, or freedom as power. This is the case because the idea that we can attain freedom as power by means of incessant human rights-based political activism without or beyond the role of strong, efficient and properly representative government is to miss the wood for the trees. The substance of many human rights may articulate some

---

[61] J. Locke, *Two Treatises on Government* (Cambridge: Cambridge University Press, 1988 [1689]).
[62] J. S. Mill, *On Liberty and Other Essays*, ed. John Gray (Oxford: Oxford University Press, 2008 [1859]).
[63] J. Rawls, *Theory of Justice* (Cambridge, MA: Harvard University Press, 1971); J. Rawls, *Political Liberalism* (New York: Columbia University Press, 1996).

of the substance of real modern freedom, but the discourse provides no guide as to how these substantive goals may best be achieved and maintained, especially when mobilized against realistic citizen agency through effective political representation. My claim here is that the institutional means of generating real freedom as power for all citizens (and some other necessary components of freedom as power) can only be achieved and maintained through empowering forms of political representation. Human rights discourse is deleterious to our felicitous understanding and formatting of a politics that empowers in this sense as it misses this all-important point. Moreover, it makes citizens think they haven't missed the point at all; it makes them *feel* powerful even under conditions when they have no meaningful political agency and representation. Human rights therefore often make people feel as if they have real political agency, when in fact they have very little power at all. 'Human rights are the modern form of opiate for politically neutered populations.'[64]

Leaving civil society activists and discourse to one side, what should be even more concerning for South Africans is the fact that the lauded National Development Plan, a plan drawn up in 2011 by the newly created National Planning Commission and adopted by the ANC government to reduce poverty to zero and unemployment to 6% by 2030, also expresses the same kind of naiveté. It formulates the main task as 'creating a virtuous cycle of expanding opportunities, building capacities, reducing poverty … all leading to rising living standards' and claims that 'such a virtuous cycle requires *agreement* across society about the contributions and sacrifices of all sectors and interests … *in the new story every citizen is concerned about the wellbeing of all other citizens*'. 'We must build our social solidarity' it submits, as the basis of reaching the ambitious targets it sets.[65] The emphasis on agreement, that all should be concerned with the well-being of everyone else and the basis for this is social solidarity, seems to me and a few other critics as nothing more than wishful thinking.[66] Given existing power relations and forms of economic and political representation, agreement or consensus is completely unrealistic, as it is in most forms of political or collective action. To expect, for example, the extremely well-remunerated master (most are male) of the powerful corporate enterprise within the infamous core of South Africa's economy – the Minerals Energy Complex (MEC) – or the newly empowered, enriched ANC politician to sacrifice some

[64] Geuss and Hamilton, 'Human Rights', p. 103.
[65] Cited in S. Terreblanche, *Lost in Transformation: South Africa's Search for a New Future since 1986* (Johannesburg: KMM Review Publishing, 2012), p. 116–117.
[66] S. Terreblanche, *Lost in Transformation*, p. 118.

component of their power and wealth without being compelled to do so is pie
in the sky. It rests on a completely unrealistic assumption regarding human
motivation – that humans in general are driven more by civic duty than by self-
interest – that, ironically, has pervaded the arguments and propositions of many
of the more astute and progressive minds in South Africa's history, not least
of the famous claim made by Mandela discussed in this book's introduction:
'For to be free is not merely to cast off one's chains but to live in a way that
respects and enhances the freedom of others'.[67] More exactly, there are three
main unrealistic assumptions that underpin the human rights discourse, Nelson
Mandela's vision and the National Development Plan: that consensus is possible
over the set of interests or rights that will generate freedom for all; that sacrifice
and civic duty are necessary for their realization; and that therefore both depend
upon unity and solidarity amongst all citizens. All three assumptions are very
wide off the mark: consensus is unlikely, duty is unnecessary and solidarity is
dangerous for the simple reason that the needs and interests of South Africans,
as are those of citizens in most polities worldwide, are not only extremely diverse
but the satisfaction of one group's or class's needs and interests – let's say the
poor and unemployed in South Africa – are likely to be in direct conflict with
the satisfaction of the needs, interests and rights of another group or class, for
instance, those of the masters of the MEC. The National Development Plan ends
up in a terrain of unrealistic platitudes because it fails to take this seriously; and
fails to do so because it does not analyse or even consider the historic trends of the
past 130 years or more, especially regarding the perpetuation of skewed power
relations and forms of economic and political representation that underpin the
dire problems of poverty, unemployment and inequality analysed in Chapter 2.

Conclusion

As I have argued in this chapter, the possible outcomes of the distorted forms
of representation that prevail in contemporary South Africa are revolution
or a successful decoupling of the alliance and the institution of effective and
meaningful representation for all groups. To avoid revolution, South Africa must
change now the power relations that exist between groups, their representatives
and the people's formal political representatives; in order to do so, it has to

---

[67] N. Mandela, *Long Walk to Freedom: The Autobiography of Nelson Mandela* (Johannesburg:
Macdonald Purnell, 1995), p. 617.

transform not only its electoral system and the structure of its ruling party, but also its property ownership, distributive mechanisms and macroeconomic policies. I only discussed the first few steps in this argument here, though; the rest are discussed in Chapter 4, especially as regards macroeconomic management.

My main submission in this chapter, is that few will even begin to see what is necessary to generate freedom through representation in South Africa unless and until representative democracy is understood in terms not just of a relation of individual and state autonomy for freedom and representation, but also of *group freedom and group representation, linked together via an account of freedom as power, in particular the power of individuals and groups to determine their economies and polities via the relative power of their representatives.*[68] I also argued that the discourse of human rights, although central to the liberation of South Africa from apartheid, now acts as an ideological foil, giving South Africans the sense of real political agency, when in fact they have none or at least very little.

In the concluding chapter I provide a series of specific institutional suggestions for South Africa regarding how best to bring about freedom as power through political representation, especially given this and the next chapter's diagnosis of the disease that cripples South Africa.

---

[68] 'It is in the selection of economic policies that in peacetime the holders of modern state power most crucially exert the impress of human understanding and will on the actual life chances of those they rule.' Dunn, 'Representation and Good Government in Africa', p. 156.

4

Elite Compromise

How could so much hope following the fall of apartheid be dashed so quickly and with such devastating social and economic effects? Why did an optimistic period of political liberation and transition to democracy give rise to a macro-political structure with so little hope for generating real freedom? The answer, as always, is in the detail, in this case, the detail of the particular history of the transition to democracy and the detail of macroeconomic policy choices, the detail of a compromise amongst National Party (NP) and African National Congress (ANC) elites that maintained existing economic power relations rather than enabling their transformation and thus the transformation of existing power relations in the polity *and* the economy. As I shall argue in this chapter, the elite compromise was the result of a complex coincidence of interests and a lack of leadership in the face of the predominant global discourses of the day regarding how best to manage the economy in order to ensure, the new political leadership thought, the credibility of the post-apartheid state. They assumed incorrectly that conformity to these norms and discourses would be necessary and sufficient means of securing the necessary inflows of international capital or foreign direct investment (FDI). An unfortunate corollary of this, moreover, was that for all the talk of transformation in South Africa, systemically there has been little or no transformation of the highly unequal power relations and distribution of property and opportunity – the main legacies of how Dutch and British colonial administrations and the apartheid government accommodated themselves to corporate power in South Africa.[1] The elite compromise was counterproductive in the following two related senses. Given the inadequate response to socio-economic and political power relations that it entailed, the result has been quite the opposite of that intended: (a) the old economic elite,

---

[1] S. Terreblanche, *The History of Inequality in South Africa: 1652–2002* (Pietermaritzburg: University of Natal Press, 2002); S. Terreblanche, *Lost in Transformation* (Johannesburg: KMM Review Publishing, 2012), ch. 3.

only partially in the process of being transformed, do not have sufficient formal representation in parliament and so cannot act as a veto on policy formation, which generates uncertainty for investors in South Africa or South African government bonds; (b) unresolved social cleavages based on extreme levels of inequality and unemployment generate violent conflicts or the constant threat of them and their brutal repression, which exacerbates economic uncertainty. What follows is that South Africa remains a risky place in which to invest, at least in the eyes of potential international investors.

There is little doubt that the heady days of the end of apartheid were days of *extreme* uncertainty, periodic outbreaks of bloodletting on a scale bordering on civil war and palpable fear regarding the possibility of a peaceful future for South Africa. It is understandable, therefore, that the minds of the leaders of both opposing parties, the ANC as spearhead of the liberation movement and the NP as the government in power, were focused on stability, that is, on generating a *peaceful* transition to a *peaceful* democratic South Africa. Moreover, as discussed in the first chapter of this book, the international context was also important: the end of the cold war, the unchecked rise of liberal, constitutional, free-market democracies, the discourse of human rights, judicial review and associated legitimization of unelected courts as sources and soundboards for legislation. The result was an agreement or compromise between these two negotiating parties that fell in line with these demands, discourses and desires of the day and safeguarded the two main sets of interests of both parties: that private property and the supposedly very distinct 'cultural' groups would be safeguarded by a formal, equal and constitutional framework; that the election of political representatives would occur by some means of majority rule or popular democracy (without group rights to ensure a 'white' veto); and that political power would remain centralized around the party in power. The first was vital for NP acceptance and the second and third for ANC assent. The first set of components was secured by means of human rights and strong extra-political legal mechanisms such as the sovereignty of the constitution, judicial review and justiciable rights for all; and the second two were safeguarded via the electoral system of closed party list proportional representation, as discussed in Chapter 3.

In this chapter, I begin with a short historical account of the two components of this compromise: the political and the economic. I argue that the compromise was made in the interests of both sets of elites and at the expense of the interests of the majority of the population. A very important element of this was the decision taken, ultimately, by the ANC that they should *not* renege on apartheid debt and they should not risk frightening away the economic representatives of existing and potential domestic and foreign investors. As exemplified in their management of public debt since 1994, they swallowed hook, line and sinker the economic orthodoxies of the age, in order they thought to enhance their sovereign power. The tragic irony of this decision is that not only has the exact opposite been the case – they now have less, not more, sovereign power – but it was made at the expense of righting the wrongs of the past through redistribution and the recalibration of power relations, that is, at the expense of the well-being and freedom of the majority of previously disadvantaged South Africans. As has been argued throughout, the freedom as power of most South Africans has, if anything, worsened since the end of apartheid. The inhumane and illegitimate regime of apartheid has been replaced by an equally inhumane if formally legitimate regime. The average South African citizen therefore has every reason to feel let-down, frustrated and angered by the ANC as political party in power, its erstwhile liberator. Whether the citizenry will, in the near future, be motivated to vote them out of power is another question entirely. For various complex reasons, mostly due to lack of power, information and the persistence of tradition in voting patterns, a positive answer to that question seems doubtful, though the results of the 2014 election may provide some interesting indicators.

Political compromise

The final, formal process of negotiation occurred over the substance of the Constitution, which was initially called the Multi-Party Negotiating Process (MPNP) and began on 1 April 1993 at the World Trade Centre, Kempton Park, and ended with the ratification of the South African Constitution on 10 December 1996 at Sharpeville, the scene of the notorious massacre on 21 March 1960, when the South African police opened fire on a crowd of 'black' protesters, killing 69 people. Despite the sharp disagreement and fraught negotiations over a number of central issues, for example, whether the constitution should include a bill of rights and whether that should itself include a right to property, the final outcome was claimed a 'very progressive document' founded on human rights and dignity for all with a bill of rights that does include a right to property.[2]

---

[2] L. M. Du Plessis, 'A Background to Drafting the Chapter on Fundamental Rights', in *Birth of a Constitution*, ed. de Villiers (Cape Town: Juta & Co, 1994), pp. 89–100; A. J. van der Walt, 'Property Rights, Land Rights, and Environmental Rights', in *Rights and Constitutionalism: The New South African Legal Order*, ed. van Wyk *et al.* (Oxford: Clarendon Press, 1996), pp. 455–501; R. Spitz and M. Chaskalson, *The Politics of Transition: A Hidden History of South Africa's Negotiated Settlement* (Oxford: Hart, 2000); L. Hamilton, *The Political Philosophy of Needs* (Cambridge: Cambridge University Press, 2003); and L. Hamilton and N. Viegi Debt, 'Democracy and Representation in South Africa', *Representation*, 45.2 (2009), pp. 193–212.

During these constitutional negotiations, South African political and economic leaders seemed to have little option but to compromise on a number of fundamental matters. As has been argued elsewhere, even the framework itself was a very significant compromise, particularly in the light of ANC's avowed positions and the substance of its Freedom Charter, the statement of core principles of the ANC and its allies, officially adopted on 26 June 1955 in Kliptown. Thus, at a time of rapid historical transformation the constitution immunized against change a bill of rights, judicial review, and a number of extra-legislative or extra-parliamentary institutions for 'supporting democracy', known as the 'chapter nine institutions', such as the Human Rights Commission, whose structures and goals are outlined in Chapter 9 of the 1996 constitution.[3]

However, it is important to note that clandestine negotiations had begun as early as 1986, involving exiled members of the ANC and representatives of more liberal and academic components of the Afrikaner political establishment and some of the significantly more Anglophone captains of industry, in particular, those that controlled the core of South Africa's Minerals Energy Complex (MEC).[4] Despite his release of Nelson Mandela and the unbanning of all previously banned parties, in 1990 president de Klerk explicitly rejected the principle of majority rule advanced by the ANC, and proposed the idea of group rights to ensure a 'white' veto. Thus initial, seemingly intractable opposition arose around two opposing concepts: power-sharing and majority rule. The logjam was broken by the ANC proposal for an all-party congress to negotiate the route to a constituent assembly. This paved the way for the Convention for a Democratic South Africa (CODESA One), convened in December 1991 and attended by 280 delegates from 19 political parties. Here

---

[3] L. Hamilton, 'Human Needs, Land Reform and the South African Constitution', *Politikon*, 33.2 (2006), pp. 133–145; and for problems with the fact that constitutions immunize against change interests and power relations that obtain in a particular time and place; and that in order to shield present and future generations from the unchecked power of past generations and accept that reason is subject to error and change over time, and thus that it is important to presume the need for permanent revision to the constitution, see marquis de Condorcet, *Foundations of Social Choice and Political Theory*, trans., ed. I. McLean and F. Hewitt, 3–90 (Aldershot: Edward Elgar, 1994), pp. 410–411, 340–341; various letters from Thomas Jefferson to many other leading public figures, between 1789 and 1824, in T. Jefferson, *The Papers of Thomas Jefferson*, ed. J. P. Boyd et al. (Princeton: Princeton University Press, 1950–); J. Waldron, *Law and Disagreement* (Oxford: Oxford University Press, 1999); J. Waldron, *The Dignity of Legislation* (Cambridge: Cambridge University Press, 1999); S. Tsoeu-Ntokoane, 'The Politics of Constitutionalism in South Africa: Institutions Supporting Democracy', unpublished University of Johannesburg DPhil Thesis.

[4] For details on these various figures and their machinations, see R. Harvey, *The Fall of Apartheid: The Inside Story from Smuts to Mbeki*, 2nd revised edition (London: Palgrave, 2003); B. Turok, *From The Freedom Charter to Polokwane: The Evolution of ANC Economic Policy* (Cape Town: New Agenda, 2008); Terreblanche, *Lost in Transformation* and M. Gevisser, *The Dream Deferred: Thabo Mbeki* (Johannesburg: Jonathan Ball, 2007).

the important agreement was reached that there would be a two-stage process of transition, with first an interim and then, later, a final constitution. Once de Klerk had gathered a mandate to proceed with this, via a referendum amongst 'white' citizens, a second session of CODESA was then convened; however, these negotiations stalled and remained so for many months. Throughout this period there was a great deal of turbulence and violence in the country, with a particularly vicious proxy 'war' carried out between some members of the ANC and the NP government-sponsored members of the local, traditional Zulu party and the apartheid puppet government of Zululand in Natal, *Inkatha*, later to be called the Inkatha Freedom Party (IFP). The ANC also launched a programme of 'rolling mass action' – 'a series of strikes, protests and boycotts as a reminder of the mass base of the ANC's power'.[5]

However, as the veteran commentator on South African politics, Allister Sparks, put it, behind the raging tensions and conflict lay a recognition of 'mutual dependency' between the NP regime and the ANC.[6] A *bosberaad* (literally, 'bush meeting') in December 1992 enabled the development of trust and the further rise to prominence of those elements who were keen on a 'speedy transition', in particular, 'the core forces for democratic change as well as big business'.[7] And the remaining intransigence was overcome by Joe Slovo's famous defence of the need for a 'sunset clause', a case for compromise: '[A] degree of compromise will be unavoidable...the key test for the acceptability of a compromise is that it does not permanently block a future advance to non-racial democratic rule in its full connotation...compromise may be acceptable as part of an acceptable settlement package'. This 'sunset clause' was inserted into the interim constitution, providing for compulsory power-sharing for a fixed number of years and a restructuring of the civil service, taking into account existing contracts and retirement compensation.[8] The interim constitution, the details of which were determined by the MPNP, is vital for a number of reasons: it sets up the rules for power-sharing, the framework within which to hold the first democratic elections of 27 April 1994, and the general rules and principles that constrained the determination of the final constitution. In particular, it set out the guidelines for a Government of National Unity, it protected the jobs of civil

5 Turok, *Freedom Charter*, p. 42.
6 A. Sparks, *Tomorrow is Another Country* (Pretoria: Struik, 1994), p. 91, cited in Turok, *Freedom Charter*, p. 42.
7 ANC, 'Challenges of the Current Situation', Discussion Document 18 May 1993, cited in Turok, *Freedom Charter*, p. 43.
8 J. Slovo, 'Negotiations: What Room for Compromise' (mimeo), cited in Turok, *Freedom Charter*, p. 43.

servants and security personnel, it gave important powers to the nine provinces, it brought in a thoroughgoing Bill of Rights specified in the language of human rights and established a powerful constitutional court alongside guarantees of freedom of speech and the press. It was clear though that, at the end of it all, the ANC would take state power.

Within the new constitutional order, however, not only was the ANC's enactment of this power constrained by the interim constitution, but so too was the nature and substance of the final constitution of 1996, which would itself have to be written in accord with these general 'interim' principles and pressing need at the time to compromise and avoid conflict. The substance and nature of the interim and final constitutions were also, of course, heavily influenced by international discourses around constitutionalism and human rights at the time.[9] The legacy this constitutional process has left is not, however, that which was envisaged, for obvious reasons: by focusing on the needs and conflicts of the present, the constitution essentially sacrificed efficient and just government in the future for stable and prudent government in the present context of transition. (As we shall see, the same is true of the elite compromise regarding economic policy.) As Thomas Jefferson argued in another context two centuries ago, it is this inevitable fact of constitutions in general, and particularly those generated as founding documents of a newly independent polity, that is, their being documents of their day generated by 'founding fathers' focused on the present and thus with little capacity for foresight, that makes the need for periodic controlled reformulations of constitutions vital for political freedom, at least once in every generation.[10] I take this up again in the conclusion to this book, and propose a decennial constitutional plebiscite.

The results on the ground were decisions regarding the structure of the constitution and the nature of the electoral system, which were not only radical departures from their forerunners found under apartheid but, ironically, also probably the most telling bases for the lack of freedom as power through political representation in South Africa today. The first decision, in an overly literal application of the doctrine of the rule of law, makes the constitution sovereign; articulates the means and goals within the constitution using a set

---

[9] H. Klug, *Constituting Democracy: Law, Globalism and South Africa's Political Reconstruction* (Cambridge: Cambridge University Press, 2000); Tsoeu-Ntokoane, 'Constitutionalism'.

[10] In various letters from Jefferson to many other leading public figures, between 1789 and 1824, in Jefferson, *The Papers of Thomas Jefferson*; see also, L. Hamilton, 'Human Needs and Political Judgment', in *New Waves in Political Philosophy*, ed. C. Zurn and B. de Bruin (London: Palgrave, 2009); L. Hamilton, *Freedom is Power: Liberty Through Political Representation* (Cambridge: Cambridge University Press, 2014); and footnote 3 above.

of specific, supposedly unchanging and 'compossible' human rights[11]; and entrenches mechanisms such as judicial review and extra-political institutions designed to uphold constitutional democracy in general and these rights in particular. Taken together, as I argued in Chapter 3, the effect is to undermine the significance of the country's national assembly of elected representatives, the very idea of representative democracy and thus the agency and power of South Africa's citizens.

The second decision only adds injury to insult in this regard. It is the decision regarding the best electoral system for a free, democratic South Africa. Ultimately, following much negotiation, both major parties decided that it was in their interests to opt for a closed party list system of proportional representation as opposed to either the first-past-the-post Westminster model of the apartheid era or a mixed proportional representation system, in which a specified proportion of members of parliament are chosen by parties and the rest are directly elected by constituents, as is the case, for example, in Germany and Ireland. Again, as I argued in Chapter 3, this decision has had dire consequences for political representation in South Africa. A closed party list system of proportional representation undermines the power of citizens to determine who governs and in particular how they govern. It is an electoral system that does not give citizens sufficient power over their representatives (as representatives of constituencies or otherwise) and therefore cannot provide them with the relevant power over how they represent them; it also does not enable a plurality of reflections of the electorate from which the latter can choose and about which it can judge. The resultant corruption, lack of service delivery and ever-increasing levels of mistrust and discontent in South Africa are manifestations of this lack of political freedom.

Ironically, the internationalization of the anti-apartheid movement not only helped generate the negotiated transition to democracy between two old foes – the NP and the ANC – but also, combined with the power *impasse* between them, helped generate an elite compromise: the replacement of one political elite with another, cosmetic political and economic changes that deferred to the interests and concerns of the present and the need for domestic and international capital and FDI at the expense of meaningful redistribution and institutional reconfigurations to address properly the injustices of the past.

---

[11] Contemporary libertarians argue that genuine rights are compossible in the sense that they yield a set, the members of which cannot yield conflicting verdicts, that is, properly construed, rights do not conflict with one another. H. Steiner, 'Essay on Rights', *Canadian Journal of Philosophy*, 26.2 (June 1996).

The desire by the two main players in the negotiated transition and during the early years of democratic rule to avoid violence – to avoid another Sharpeville or Soweto – is central to understanding the kind of democracy and freedom that this period generated for South Africa. The prudence or extreme caution of both main negotiating parties has left an unfortunate political and economic legacy for contemporary South Africa: extreme orthodoxy as regards macroeconomic policy and forms of economic and political representation that enable elite power at the price of the empowerment of South African citizens in general. And both betray the mark of strong international forces: in having become so internationalized, the nature of the problem in South Africa, although in some sense vital for keeping South Africa one step removed from the vertigo of violence, also constrained its capacity to generate novel political and economic institutions and policy that might really transform an otherwise very warped and unequal society, economy and polity. That South Africans have had to live and die through another massacre – Marikana – speaks volumes for the consequences of this elite compromise: Marikana provides such vivid echoes of Sharpeville, not just because it was a massacre perpetrated by police on downtrodden citizens, but also because it laid bare the cooptation amongst democratic South Africa's economic and political elites, an elite compromise that has worsened rather than reduced the potential for social cleavages, conflict and destruction.[12]

Economic compromise

It is characteristic of the many waves of decolonization and national independence that they are followed by a process of extensive borrowing in order to fuel economic growth and development. In 1994 the new South African government bucked this trend. It had inherited an economy in disarray and the new political elites had before them three possible options. First, they could default on apartheid debt. Second, they could refinance existing debt with more debt from international institutions to address the urgent issues of income redistribution and economic transformation. Third, they could seek to stabilize the economy and reduce public debt by adopting an austere fiscal programme. They chose

---

[12] *Cf.* The arguments put forward towards the end of the apartheid period in the academic journal *Politikon*, the broader grey press and amongst many of the old guard who were wary of real change regarding consociation between elites as a means of avoiding cleavages and conflict amongst countries in transition to democracy, drawing especially on A. Lijphart, *The Politics of Accommodation* (Berkeley: University of California Press, 1975); A. Lijphart, *Democracy in Plural Societies* (New Haven: Yale University Press, 1977).

the third option. Why did they make this decision and how has it shaped the political and economic development of democratic South Africa?

The choice was made in order to gain greater policy independence from creditors and portray an image of sound fiscal management to potential international investors. In accordance with the predominant economic orthodoxy regarding representative democracy, public debt and state credibility, the new South African elite assumed that a combination of secure institutions of representative democracy and 'prudent' monetary and fiscal management would enhance the state's credibility and thus make it less expensive for them to finance the transformation of South Africa's economy. However, the consequences of the decision were quite the opposite. The South African government's austere response to debt made its bonds more attractive. It has therefore become more, not less, dependent on the constraints of creditors, that is, more subject to investor scrutiny and sentiment. And, yet, the brutal irony is that, in the eyes of investors, South Africa still lacks creditworthiness and remains a relatively risky place in which to invest, and thus, relative to other young representative democracies, the servicing of South Africa's public debt remains expensive.

Parallel to the formal debate around the nature of the rules that would, ultimately, be codified in the new, final constitution of 1996 and the related forms of political representation, particularly as regards the legislature and the executive, there was a semi-formal or informal debate in which national economic power – particularly that of the leaders in the MEC and banking sector – and the new political elite defined an economic 'constitution' that would characterize the new South Africa. Clandestine discussions in this 'forum' began as early as 1986 and, over time, generated an economic compromise that included forms of representation and a parcelling out of the main economic powers and interests in South Africa in a highly problematic fashion: a form of commercial representation of the main economic powers and interests in South Africa that had dire consequences for both economic growth and transformation in South Africa. This is the second under-discussed compromise and form of representation that, I maintain, determine to a significant degree the extent to which South Africans lack freedom today. Given the transformation in political power, it was clear to most of those involved in the negotiated settlement that the interests of the existing economic elite, at least initially, would not be represented in parliament. Although the constitution of 1996 provided a legal safeguard for the general interests of the economic elite, in the form of a right to property, in and of itself it did not ensure that the main economic powers could retain effective control over the economy. Their effective control over the economy was secured or at least bolstered by an informal agreement between these parties, that is, between the new political elite and the old economic elite, not entirely unlike the consensus of post-1948 South Africa between big business and the new Afrikaner political elite. This agreement was made possible by the fact that it became obvious very quickly to all involved that the old economic elite held a vital card: they constituted the majority of the existing creditors for the South African state and their credit was a basic prerequisite for a stable, if transforming, South Africa.

And, yet, the harsh ironic reality is that, in the eyes of investors, South Africa still lacks creditworthiness and remains a relatively risky place in which to invest, and thus, relative to other young representative democracies, the servicing of South Africa's public debt remains expensive.[13] In other words, both of the two main pillars of this informal agreement failed to sustain the conditions for the attainment of the intended objectives of the original decision regarding public debt. South Africa's creditworthiness has not improved and the new South African government does not have greater control over policy formation. Rather the prudent management of public debt and the policy priority given to equilibrium and fiscal and monetary discipline simply safeguarded the interests of the existing creditor class (and the interests of potential investors) to the detriment of social spending, redistribution and transformation.

The behind-the-scenes agreements, assurances and concessions that were made during this period provided the necessary means to ensure that monetary and fiscal policy would not undermine the interests of those who had the means and potential to continue to act as creditors for the South African state. The quick and sorry demise of the ANC's 'Making Democracy Work' policy is a case in point, indicative of the way in which the elite economic compromise sacrificed many of the ANC's previously stated goals for the perceived absolute priority to secure monetary and fiscal policy that was attractive to international markets. 'Making Democracy Work' was a policy proposal produced by the ANC-sponsored Macroeconomic Research Group (MERG) in November 1993. As an attempt to turn the general promises of the Freedom Charter – for housing and health care – into practical policies, it was the most important research base for the ANC in the early stages of its unbanning.[14] However, it only operated between 1991 and 1993 and most of its policy proposals never saw the light of day. The whole project was dropped as part of the horse-trading that constituted

---

[13] Hamilton and Viegi, 'Democracy and Representation in South Africa'.
[14] Macroeconomic Research Group, *Making Democracy Work: A Framework for Macroeconomic Policy in South Africa* (Cape Town: Centre for Development Studies, 1993).

the negotiations between the representatives of the old economic elite and the new political elite.[15] The same fate befell the first economic policy of the ANC government, the Reconstruction and Development Policy (RDP), a document that had been heavily influenced by MERG. Some have argued that the ANC leadership was simply outmanoeuvred in these negotiations.[16] This may, in part, be true, but even as they make this argument, these commentators provide evidence for the ANC's active involvement in this process. Take, for example, the central role played by Thabo Mbeki, who made several key revisions to the ANC's economic programme to address the concerns of top business people and industrialists, such as Harry Oppenheimer, in all likelihood with the approval of Nelson Mandela, who was not exempt from the allures of the latter's riches – the two meeting frequently for lunch and dinner in this period.[17]

In terms of representation, the main economic agents – the top business people and industrialists – essentially act as informal representatives of existing and potential national creditors (and owners of capital more generally). In other words, those individuals who have the means to purchase South African government bonds *identify* with the main economic agents and thus feel that their interests are being represented by them. This is very important as the market or, more exactly, potential creditors respond to whether or not their interests will be defended within the formal structures of a state's representative democracy. If they feel they will be, they feel less uncertain about the course of future macroeconomic policy and thus more willing to invest than they would otherwise. Their interests can be defended either by representatives from parties that enjoy the support of (potential) creditors or by representatives with whom they identify, but who may not formally represent creditor interests. In both cases, the creditors can only be sure that their interests are being accorded *political* representation if their agents or the representative with whom they identify are members of the formal institutions of political representation, that is, are members of parliament. What is peculiar in the case of South Africa is not the presence of this kind of representation, but the fact that this group of representatives is relatively homogeneous and it did not expect to be represented

---

[15] N. Nattrass, 'Politics and Economics in ANC Economic Policy', *African Affairs*, 93 (1994), pp. 343–359.

[16] N. Klein, *The Shock Doctrine* (London: Penguin, 2007), pp. 200–206; W. Gumede, *Thabo Mbeki and the Battle for the Soul of the ANC* (Cape Town: Zebra Press, 2005).

[17] On Mbeki, see Gumede, *Battle for the Soul*, pp. 33, 39; on Mandela, see Terreblanche, *Lost*, ch 4; and for more on the political economic motivations behind the shift in economic policy of the ANC towards an orthodox fiscal and monetary management, see A. Habib and V. Padayachee, 'Economic Policy and Power in South Africa's Transition to Democracy', *World Development*, 28.2 (2000), pp. 245–263.

in parliament, that is, by the democratically elected political elite. In fact, the interests of the old economic elite, whose continued support and presence as creditors are vital for economic stability and state credibility, are still represented by the small number of relatively homogeneous economic agents at the helm of South Africa's economy, especially in the financial and MEC sectors.[18] Aware that they were unlikely to have their interests represented in parliament, they ensured that the constitution of 1996 secured these interests in its vaunted bill of rights, a set of rules for South Africa's nascent representative democracy that safeguards universal suffrage without seriously jeopardizing the economic power of capital in general and national creditors in particular.

South Africa is unusual as a result of the manner in which the main economic and political representatives have been marked by its history of racial discrimination: the economic elite is homogeneous in the sense that it was then and still is largely dominated by a relatively small group of 'white' capitalists, industrialists and families and it did not expect to be represented within parliament. At least in terms of local and international perception, the new ANC government would first and foremost represent the interests of the previously disenfranchised 'black' majority. (Whether in fact the ANC now comes even close to defending the interests and helping to meet the needs of the previously disenfranchised is doubtful.) The predominantly 'white' economic elite may have courted and been courted by the new predominantly 'black' political representatives, but it could not assume that its interests would find secure political representation within the institutions of democratic South Africa. Thus, under the current conditions, the power of these economic representative agents operates as purely economic power to a much greater extent than is the norm in other parts of the world. There are, of course, exceptions to the rule, but primarily this situation of lack of overlap, as it were, between economic and political representatives is more obvious and stark in the case of South Africa as a consequence of the extent to which it is still an issue of race: the policy of Black Economic Empowerment (BEE) only really runs skin deep; it has added a few 'black' figureheads, but has yet to transform the identity as a whole of the representatives of economic power in South Africa, that is, the CEOs of the relatively few large firms that dominate the South African economy.[19]

---

[18] For details, see Turok, *Freedom Charter* and Terreblanche, *Lost.*
[19] See Terreblanche, *Lost,* chs 4 & 5 for the identity of the main controllers of the South African economy, especially the MEC, that is, those individuals who constitute the bulk of domestic creditors and representatives for potential international investors: still predominantly 'white'.

South Africa's inability to gain the levels of creditworthiness that ought to have been the result of constituting representative democracy is explained by one of the main consequences of the negotiated settlement: the economic elite does not enjoy formal, political representation and thus does not control a 'veto point'. In other words, it does not have strict veto power over political decision-making. (A 'veto point' is a political institution, the holder of which, as specified by a country's constitution, has the power to block a proposed change in policy.[20]) International investors also thereby lack a 'veto point', as the domestic economic elite represent their interests, in the sense that they identify with one another's interests, and thus they deem South Africa a risky place in which to invest. The uncertainty generated by the fact that the economic elite are not in formal control of a veto point is only made worse by the inability of existing economic policy effectively to redistribute and recalibrate power relations sufficiently to empower the citizenry as a whole and thus reduce the possibility of often violent industrial action, service delivery strikes and general discontent. The fact that the new political elite does not transform macroeconomic policy to attain these ends is a complex historical matter that has to do with the lack of accountability in the macro-political structure of South Africa's democracy, the persistence of economic orthodoxies, even following the global financial crash of 2007 and its continuing aftershocks, and the continued economic dominance of financial and MEC-related capital in South Africa. That the ANC government in power is incapable or unwilling to properly confront these forces speaks volumes about its lack of courage or its poor political leadership or its sheer self-interested corruption, as it acts as not much more than a rentier class atop a distorted economy or, more likely, all three.

The orthodox argument regarding public debt and representative democracy holds that representative democracy is a necessary (and in some instances even a sufficient) condition for credibility, that is, that its institution reduces uncertainty and thus increases the value of a state's bonds, which means it becomes less expensive for a government to finance its activities.[21] The case of South Africa undermines this orthodoxy too. Since the interests of the economic elite are not *guaranteed* formal political representation within the existing, exemplary

[20] For more on 'veto points' and 'veto players', see G. Tsebelis, *Veto Players: How Political Institutions Work* (Princeton: Princeton University Press, 2002) and D. Stasavage, *Public Debt and the Birth of the Democratic State: France and Great Britain, 1688–1789* (Cambridge: Cambridge University Press, 2003).

[21] D. C. North and B. R. Weingast, 'Constitutions and Commitment: The Evolution of Institutions Governing Public Choice in Seventeenth Century England', *Journal of Economic History*, 49.4 (1989), pp. 803–832; J. Macdonald, *A Free Nation Deep in Debt: The Financial Roots of Democracy* (Princeton: Princeton University Press, 2006); *cf* Stasavage, *Public Debt*.

political institutions of representative democracy, the main group of economic representatives in South Africa constitutes a constraint on political power; they are not part and parcel of the structure of political representation. This has significant negative effects on the perception of South Africa's credibility amongst existing and potential owners of its public debt. Thus the real determining factor regarding credibility is not the institutionalization of representative democracy, but whether or not the representatives of actual and potential creditors hold the relevant formal veto points.

Stability, continuity, economic austerity and internationalization

This decision to focus on stability, continuity and economic austerity and its unintended, problematic consequences on levels of poverty, inequality and unemployment are brought out best by delving a little deeper into the details of the example of how the post-apartheid government managed public debt.

The initial outcome of the development of the new forms and dynamics of formal and informal representation discussed above was that the Mandela Government of National Unity initially retained NP appointees at the National Treasury and the South African Reserve Bank. Nelson Mandela's first treasury minister was Derek Keyes, CEO of mining group Gencor, and 'a well-known establishment personality in the apartheid era',[22] who was appointed by de Klerk, and who subsequently left after four months for personal reasons. Mandela's second treasury minister was a professional banker by the name of Chris Liebenberg, CEO of banking group Nedcor. Moreover, Chris Stals, a staunch supporter of the apartheid regime, was retained as Governor of the South African Reserve Bank. This retention of extant personnel and the character of subsequent appointments were important indicators of the desire by the ANC to stress continuity and stability.

The new ANC government focused on continuity as opposed to radical transformation for two related reasons. First, they felt the need to retain the confidence of existing domestic 'white' business people and prospective international investors. In other words, this imperative has its source in their desire to keep their side of the bargain or contract as regards fiscal policy and

---

[22] Turok, *Freedom Charter*, p. 246.

the continuity of the economic order. Second, their emphasis on continuity can also be explained by the fact that the ANC government inherited an economy in complete disarray. The levels of fiscal mismanagement of the apartheid regime from 1980 until 1994 were staggering. While GDP had grown at an average of 3.3% between 1970 and 1979, and 2.2% between 1980 and 1989, it grew at a paltry 0.2% between 1990 and 1994. Inflation had risen at an average of 14.6% between 1980 and 1989, and interest on public debt amounted to the largest budget item during this period.[23] Between 1989 and 1994, the government deficit increased from R91.2 billion ro R237 billion (in current prices), which Sampie Terreblanche regards as nothing more than 'reckless white "plundering" in the final years of white supremacy and, therefore, as another example of Afrikaner/white corruption'.[24] The ANC government took the prudent step of attempting to stabilize the ship of state first before embarking on any expansive and directly transformative policies. They decided to transform the treasury prior to flooding it with lavish borrowings.

Figure 4.1 illustrates the dynamic of total government debt in South Africa from 1970 to 2005 as percentage of GDP. From the data it is clear that the most significant accumulation of debt happened at the end of the apartheid period.

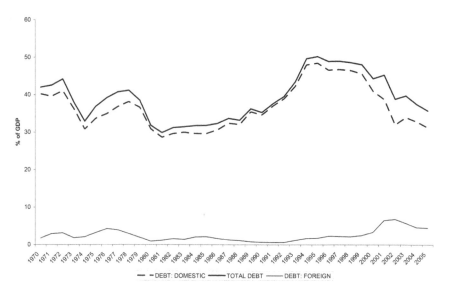

Figure 4.1 Debt dynamics in South Africa: 1970–2005

Source: International Financial Statistics

---

[23] Budget Review 2000, Available from: www.treasury.gov.za [accessed 2 November 2011].
[24] Terreblanche, *Lost*, p. 58. He goes on to claim that the question of whether the apartheid regime of 1948–1994 was more or less corrupt than the ANC government since is one that can unfortunately not be answered yet, despite popular perception that the ANC government is much more corrupt.

Nevertheless, the explosion of debt at the beginning of the 1990s has its origin in the crisis and economic policy response of the apartheid government in the 1980s. As can be seen from Figure 4.2, from the beginning of the 1980s any attempt to stabilize expenditure as a percentage of GDP had been abandoned and from 1989 revenues had fallen dramatically, creating the significant explosion of debt that the country experienced in the following years.[25]

It is also noticeable how, in the first 14 years after the end of apartheid, the effort to put public finance under control was the main driving force of Treasury policies, starting with the first annual budget of the new democratic government: note in Figure 4.2 the marked dip in expenditure in 1994.

Things began to change in 1996, at least as regards personnel. Trevor Manuel, the first 'black' Finance Minister, was appointed. His first period ran for the remaining 3 years of the Mandela government, 1996–1999, and he was in charge until the 2009 elections. The market was initially hostile to his appointment as a

Figure 4.2 Revenues and expenditure dynamics in South Africa, 1970–2010

Source: South African Reserve Bank

---

[25] E. Calitz, S. du Plessis and K. Siebrits, 'An Alternative Perspective on South Africa's Public Debt, 1962–1994', *South Journal of Economics*, Economic Society of South Africa, 79.2 (2011), pp. 161–172, show that the published record of public debt tends to attribute to the last years of apartheid a fiscal indiscipline that was actually developing much earlier, once the actuarial pension fund deficits and government debt of the apartheid homelands are considered.

consequence of racist assumptions regarding his competence as well as fears that he might begin to embark on a process of nationalization of large enterprises. In fact, on 14 June 1996, soon after his appointment, he proposed quite the opposite in the form of a new macroeconomic policy, the Growth, Employment and Redistribution (GEAR) strategy.[26] This strategy adds another vote to the 'Washington Consensus' in that it focuses on privatization, government 'right-sizing', the creation of incentives for FDI such as tariff reduction, the reduction of the fiscal deficit (which in 1994 had reached 9% of GDP) and productivity-linked wage rates.[27] Needless to mention, very soon after his first budget speech, these events allayed most of the market's fears.[28]

In other words, this part of the rationale for the choice of option three has to do with the sentiments and goals of a new regime and how these are linked to the history of debt in South Africa.[29] The new regime inherits from the apartheid regime a series of problems that are the consequence of two related legacies of apartheid: irresponsible borrowing and an over-dependence on national capital. The new political elites were intent on reversing both of these trends. They wanted to create a fiscal environment characterized by responsible borrowing that would simultaneously make South Africa attractive in the eyes of international investors – both in the sense of FDI and enhancing the creditworthiness of South African state bonds – and allow them to gain independence from national capital. Their response was an austere fiscal policy and a concomitant drop in capital expenditure and taxation, which only since 2011 is beginning to be reversed, but with little tangible and meaningful outcomes on inequality and unemployment or, indeed, infrastructure.

Coupled with this desire to gain autonomy from national capital is the hope that they could also, consequently, insure against dependence upon international financial institutions. Many of the new political leaders (often in exile) experienced decolonization in the rest of Africa and the subsequent condition of severe indebtedness of many independent African states. They had also observed the fate of populist policies and economic instability in many Latin American countries in the 1970s, the 1980s and the 1990s as one debt crisis

---

[26] T. Lodge, *Politics in South Africa: From Mandela to Mbeki* (Cape Town: David Philip, 2002), p. 26.

[27] Lodge, *Politics in South Africa*, p. 25; D. Davis, 'From the Freedom Charter to the Washington Consensus' in *The Real State of the Nation: South Africa After the 1990s, Development Update (special edition)*, ed. D. Everatt and V. Maphai, 4.3 (2003), pp. 31–48.

[28] It is ironic that the market reacted with equal nervousness when Minister Manuel announced his resignation in September 2008, at the time of President Thabo Mbeki's recall by the ANC, about which more is discussed in the main text below.

[29] See Minister Manuel's 2007 budget speech, Available from: www.treasury.gov.za [accessed 22 March 2009].

followed another. And, finally, many of them also observed firsthand the collapse of big-bang transformation policies in the former eastern block. The issue of debt and a cautious approach to transformation became central to any planning of public policies for growth and development. Thus although this is a story that has very specific South African characteristics, its origin can in part be traced back to the experiences and failures of development policies around the world in the decades before 1994. Thus the overriding motivation behind the new political leaders' choice of option three was their desire to properly harness and retain the sovereignty of the South African state, in other words, to wrench power from national creditors and avoid a loss of autonomy to international creditors and financial institutions. This claim is given extra credence by a claim made by the new governor of the Reserve Bank, Gill Marcus, who, as the then chair of Parliament's finance committee, played a central role in stabilizing the debt-ridden economy the ANC government inherited. At the time it was she who convinced her party comrades that they did not have a 'blank slate' and that if South Africa's 'huge debt' and 'massive tax shortfall' were not addressed 'it [South Africa] was likely to land up in the hands of the IMF … [and] we certainly had not worked this hard for our liberation to hand it over to the IMF'.[30] Under these conditions and given the state of the economy at the time, even with the advantage of hindsight, selecting option three seems a prudent choice.

Understood in these terms, it is easy to notice a parallel between these choices and those finally made within the constitutional process that took place within CODESA and the MPNP, culminating with the ratification of the Constitution on 10 December 1996 at Sharpeville.[31] Despite evident disagreement and fraught negotiations over whether the constitution should include a bill of rights, and whether that should itself include a right to property,[32] the final outcome was a very progressive document founded on human rights and in particular the right to property. In the final document there is some qualification of the right to property understood in terms of imperatives in line with the 'national interest', but these are to cover the need for land reform.[33] For obvious reasons, the fact

---

[30] P. Green, 'Banking on Integrity', *Mail & Guardian*, 24 July 2009; see also A. Hirsch, *Season of Hope: Economic Reform under Mandela and Mbeki* (Pietermaritzburg: University of KwaZulu-Natal Press, 2005), pp. 65–105 for a comprehensive insider analysis of the ANC economic policy in the first years of the Mandela government. As he states (p. 69), 'In order not to get too indebted to those who could turn their debt against them, they had to be conservative and pander to some of their prejudices'.

[31] T. H. R. Davenport and C. Saunders, *South Africa: A Modern History* (London: MacMillan, 2000), pp. 559–572; Spitz and Chaskalson, *The Politics of Transition*, p. xiii.

[32] For more on these matters, see Du Plessis, 'A Background to Drafting the Chapter on Fundamental Rights'; van der Walt, 'Property Rights, Land Rights, and Environmental Rights'; Spitz and Chaskalson, *The Politics of Transition*; and Hamilton, *Needs*.

[33] For more on how this has affected delivery on land reform see Hamilton, *Needs*, pp. 173–184; and Hamilton, 'Human Needs, Land Reform and the South African Constitution'.

that the right to private property is listed within the Bill of Rights was enough to satisfy the owners of capital. Thus the form of the final constitution of 1996 is very much determined by the perceived need to safeguard the interests (property) of the capital-owning class; without this safeguard this class and the old elite under which it had flourished would not have lent their support to the new political elite. As I have argued, since the outgoing elite were unlikely to be represented within the incoming majority ANC government, the constitution offered them the main means of safeguarding their interests.

This is clearly evident with regard to the right to property. Although the constitution provides a comprehensive list of individual entitlements or rights that the framers determined would be necessary for transformation, the ability to actualize these rights depends upon resources and their distribution. For example, in order for a new citizen without property to make proper use of these enshrined rights, in particular the right to property, they must first acquire property. The constitution stipulates a right of access to property, but this is weak in the face of a similarly enshrined right to property (both in clause 25 of the Bill of Rights) as well as a well-entrenched property-owning status quo. The only realistic means by which a new citizen without property can acquire property is if fiscal policy ensures the redistribution of property. However, if the nation's debt and wealth are concentrated within the small group of property owners whose interests are likely to be directly affected by this kind of policy, as is the case in South Africa, they are likely to make use of their unique position of power to hinder the process of property redistribution. As a consequence of what this entails, they will therefore act in a manner counter to transformation and the general actualization of rights: they own the debt and ensure that fiscal policy follows an equilibrium path, which they themselves define. In other words, so long as they retain the debt, they retain the power to discipline the government by dint of the fact that the state cannot function without their credit. All governments need creditors, even under conditions of austerity, and so creditors are in a privileged position as regards the formation of fiscal policy. Therefore in a national context, the only way to transform under these conditions is either to default on debt; expropriate property and distribute; or gain a modicum of independence from national lenders by reducing indebtedness. The new ANC government chose the last, most conservative option, with the goal of eventually placing sovereignty in the hands of all of the citizenry, if its rhetoric is anything to go by. But in doing so, it surrendered the only effective means of enabling the rest of society to actualize their rights, for without redistribution they remain in a condition in which they are lacking the resources to do so. The hope is that the process of 'transformation through austerity' would generate, 'in the end', sufficient growth to eliminate any distributional constraint. However, this depends on two unstable variables – growth and continued economic sovereignty. And, as John Maynard Keynes famously put it: 'But this *long run* is a misleading guide to current affairs. *In the long run* we are all dead'.[34]

The alternative options of reneging on apartheid debt and accessing aggressively international official financial institutions to finance economic and social reform were not considered feasible. The choice of cautious reform is actually quite unique in the context of dramatic political and economic regime change. At least since the French Revolution, history is replete with examples of shock therapies, often involving reneging on debt, radical land reform, nationalization (or privatization) of natural resources, in general radical and fast changes in economic and political institutions. In the case of South Africa, the imposition of shock therapy would have been to disregard the constraints imposed by the main economic representatives and their 'constituents' and promote economic equality through land reform and debt cancellation. The price might have been economic isolation and stagnation for a considerable period of time, although the chance that this would have been the result must be tempered by odious debt considerations and the fact of significant international goodwill following the end of apartheid in South Africa.[35] Moreover, the potential benefits of this admittedly more risky option would have been so great that they would have outweighed the risks. The conservative choice of option three, in contrast, constituted a decision in favour of stability, continuity, austerity, internationalization and the delegation of economic oversight to a yet-to-be-transformed economic elite.[36] Until this elite, or at least its representatives,

---

[34] J. M. Keynes, *A Tract on Monetary Reform* (London: MacMillan and Co., 1923), p. 80.

[35] 'Odious debts' are debts that have been incurred by a government that was not democratically chosen, and the borrowed money might even have helped a brutal regime stay in power. Given this, considerations of situations of odious debt marshal the associated moral case for debt forgiveness, maintaining that the citizens of countries under these regimes, especially once they are no longer in power, ought not be saddled with the debt incurred by these regimes, for example, Mobutu's regime in Congo, Pinochet's regime in Chile and that of apartheid South Africa – in other words, there exists a strong moral argument that South Africa in transition had no moral obligation to repay the debts incurred under apartheid. P. Adams, *Odious Debts: Loose Lending, Corruption, and the Third World's Environmental Legacy* (Oxford: Earthscan Publications, 1991); J. Stiglitz, *Making Globalization Work* (London: Penguin, 2007).

[36] Ronnie Kasrils, ANC veteran and a government minister until 2008, bemoans this last move in particular:

I was as guilty as others in focusing on my own responsibilities and government portfolios and leaving the economic issues to the ANC experts. This was a dire error and I believe we are paying for such a lapse at huge cost. Too often both the revolutionary soldier and political

is completely transformed, this choice also ensures that the representatives of creditors are unlikely also to be represented in the formal structures and institutions of the government; in other words, it ensures that they do not acquire a power of veto over government policy, unless of course they are given access via other means, such as the electoral success of a party that does formally represent their interests.

Increased credibility?

The choice made in 1994 saw economic discipline and austerity as one of the main means of consolidating representative democracy and thus increasing the credibility of the South African state. In this sense the new political elite were partially correct. In doing so South Africa has successfully structured its economy in a manner that gives rise to an increase in its creditworthiness. One of the main indicators of accountability and credibility for financial investors is the existence of consolidated institutions of representative democracy.

Two important things follow from this state of affairs. First, the South African government has managed to acquire the kind of independence in its policymaking that it was seeking: 'The managers of public finance do not need to serve other masters than those to whom they profess loyalty'.[37] Therefore, spending in service delivery to the general population, education, housing and social protection has increased exponentially, at least of late. However, second, the internationalization of the economy produced by the increase of creditworthiness has meant that the actions and decisions of the South African government are now regulated and disciplined to a much greater extent by the interests and sentiments of international market participants. The state has no sovereign relation to these investors and most are, obviously, not citizens and are therefore not represented formally within any of the institutions that constitute representative democracy in South Africa. They are not even part of the informal national economic forum that produced the economic compromise before and post 1994. The only relation that exists is through markets and the sentiments

---

activist leave economic affairs to the specialists. My greatest mistake is having neglected economic study. Would-be revolutionaries need to wake up every morning and exclaim: 'It's the economy, stupid! Understand it!'.

R. Kasrils, *Armed & Dangerous: From Undercover Struggle to Freedom*, updated edition (Johannesburg: Jacana, 2013), p xxiv.

[37] Lodge, *Politics in South Africa*, p. 25.

and moods that affect these markets. This was not what was intended. The programme of austerity was chosen specifically as the best means of securing greater independence for the new South African government, but the result is in fact increased interdependence on the conditions of other emerging markets and the sentiments of international investors.

The measure that best maps the historical events that we have described is derived from the analysis of the fluctuations of the yield curve on government bonds.[38] Put simply, the idea is that a change in political or economic expectations will have an effect on the evaluation of the same asset at different dates of maturity. If the market expects a political crisis, long-term investment will be more risky relative to short-term investment, thus affecting the relative returns. Using this property of the yield curve of government debt, we estimate a measure based on the deviation of the yield curve from the long-term equilibrium relationship and we call it a time varying risk premium.[39] In Figure 4.3, the solid line is the time-varying risk measure on South African government bonds from 1981 to 2007, whereas the dotted line is the underlying short-run fluctuations from which this

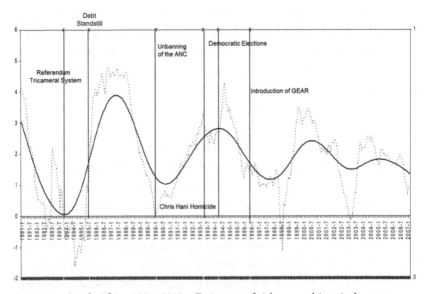

Figure 4.3 South Africa 1981–2007 – Estimates of risk versus historical events

---

[38] For technical details, see J. Fedderke and N. Pillay, 'A Theoretically Defensible Measure of Risk: Using Financial Market Data from a Middle Income Context', *ERSA Working Paper*, No. 64 (2007). Essentially the measure extracts a risk measure from the co-integrating relationship between yields at different maturity. The time-varying risk premium is chosen for its ability to match historical events as shown in Figure 4.3.

[39] I say 'we' here and in what follows as the remainder of this section is taken from research Nicola Viegi and I produced together. I would have been at sea without his technical knowhow.

measure is derived through a process of filtering. The solid line is derived using a Hodrick–Prescott filter on the residuals of the co-integrating relationships between three months, three years and ten years of government bond yields. The vertical lines represent historical events that help evaluate the ability of this risk measure to capture the real market response to events. So, for example, the tricameral referendum of 1983 seemed to be a period of relatively good evaluation by the creditors of the prospect of the country. This impression was very rapidly reversed with the dramatic increase in political conflict in the second half of the 1980s and with the debt standstill in 1985. The legalization of the ANC seems to have been another moment of relative optimism, followed by the uncertainty of the pre-election period. After the election, and especially with the introduction of GEAR in 1996, we observe a process of stabilization of expectations with a series of fluctuations in correspondence with international economic uncertainty.

We submit that this measure captures quite well past political and economic uncertainty. If this is the case, how do we evaluate the volatility and overall risk? The most important thing to note is that even following political stabilization, the country is still evaluated with a degree of suspicion by international markets. Although the average fluctuation seems to be reducing, especially after the second election in 1999, it is still substantially different from any concept of an equilibrium relationship. The mean risk today is still very similar to the mean risk prior to 1994.

A useful comparison is the one between our market risk measures and political risk measures we find in the literature. These political risk measures, such as the Polity index, the Fedderke, De Kadt and Luiz (FKL) index (2001) or the World Bank political stability index, tend to focus on institutional stability and political conflict. As seen in Figure 4.4, the FKL index corresponds to the market index of risk we calculated for the last 10 years of apartheid. However, with the advent of democracy and the peaceful transition, institutional risk and market risk diverge considerably. Although all the indices show a marked increase in institutional quality and political stability after the introduction of democracy, the market still attaches a significant risk premium to South African debt.

Thus institutional quality tells us little about the way a country is seen by international creditors. Even the financial market 'rating' is not enough. A more directed measure of the market sentiment towards the country still shows a certain degree of caution and a significant degree of uncertainty about the country. The presence of residual uncertainty is also evident if we analyse a composite political risk index provided by the PRS group, from 1984 to 2008 as in Figure 4.5 below.

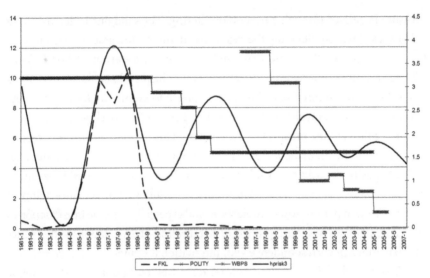

Figure 4.4 Market risk versus institutional risk
Indexes rescaled for comparsion

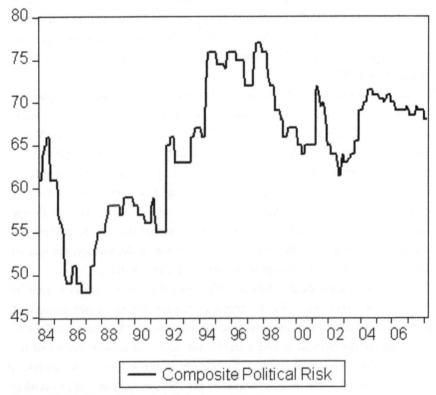

Figure 4.5 Market political risk analysis – PRS data
Source: http://www.prsgroup.com/

After a golden age of political goodwill from 1994 to 1998, market participants show persistent uncertainty about the political risk implied by social and economic indicators forming the underlying structure of the index. This political risk index is an aggregation of indicators of specific socio-economic and political indicators, namely, government stability, socio-economic conditions, investment profile, internal conflict, external conflict, corruption, military in politics, religion in politics, law and order, ethnic tensions, democratic accountability and the quality of the bureaucracy. A principal component analysis of the underlying indices shows that, while market participants recognize the stability of formal democratic institutions (which drives the first principal component of the indexes), much less progress is recognized in the fields of institutional efficiency and socio-economic transformation.

Figure 4.6 shows the two main trends in the data comprising the political stability index. The first component P1 summarizes the formal democratic gains obtained after 1994. This is certainly positive and it is seen as positive by international investors. The second component, on the other hand, summarizes the perception that South Africa is a country where socio-economic conditions,

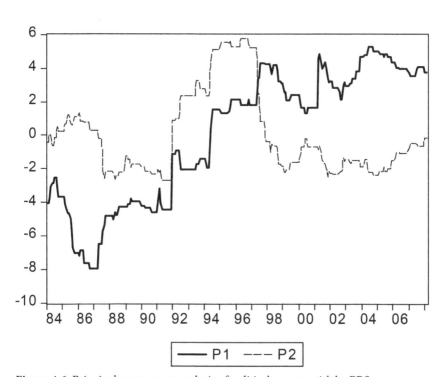

Figure 4.6 Principal component analysis of political country risk by PRS group

investment climate, corruption, crime and the quality of bureaucracy have not improved significantly or have worsened after democratization.[40]

This is important because it suggests that the government is subjected to a high degree of scrutiny by the markets.[41] And, moreover, any significant change in policies must be, as it were, 'contracted' with the market for it to be feasible; in other words, it must ensure against any negative repercussions on the credibility of the country. Independence of political power from national capital might have been achieved through fiscal discipline and economic stability, but the sovereign power required to achieve the constitutional goals is still, and is likely to continue to be, constrained by international market sentiment and approval.

An example of how prices constitute a form of judgement on government policy was the reaction of markets to Finance Minister Trevor Manuel's resignation following the 'recall' of President Thabo Mbeki by the ruling ANC party. The news provoked a strong market reaction, with 4% losses on the stock exchange, 5% devaluation of the currency and a loss of 20 basis points on government bonds. The resignation was immediately explained as a formal requirement and that Trevor Manuel was still available to serve in the new government. But the message coming from the market was clear: whatever the political instability coming from inside the ANC, the economic arrangements guaranteed by the economic policy framework established by Mr Manuel and the then reserve bank governor, Mr Mboweni, should be protected carefully, as a condition for economic stability.

Two important and related conclusions follow from this. The first is that the ANC government's intention to achieve greater independence from national and international investors had the unintended consequence of making it more,

---

[40] This perception of international investors that there is a significant political risk in South Africa was famously attacked by former President Mbeki in response to an assertion of this kind made by Mr. Trahar, CEO of Anglo American. 'Throughout the colonial and apartheid years, Anglo American did not seek a London listing, and did nothing that would generate speculation about the future of its Johannesburg Head Office. Is it now saying that democratic South Africa presents the business world and our country with higher political risk than did apartheid South Africa? What information does it have, or projections into the future, that say that there is a persisting political risk in our country, on which Anglo American must base its decisions about its future? Would the company be willing to share this information, or projections, at least with the government, so that steps could be taken to remove the risk? Is this perhaps the reason that South African companies have unusually high cash or liquid reserves, that they think that such is the level of political risk in our country, that they would be very foolish to tie up all their resources in fixed investments in our country? If this is the case, why has business not raised this matter, despite the institutionalised system of regular interaction that exists between government and business?' T. Mbeki, 'Questions that Demand an Answer', *ANC Today*, 4.36 (2004).

[41] L. Mosley, 'Constraints, Opportunities and Information: Financial Market–Government Relations around the World', in *Globalization and Egalitarian Redistribution*, ed. P. Bardhan, S. Bowles and E. Wallerstein (Princeton, NJ: Princeton University Press, 2006), pp. 87–119.

not less, dependent on the constraints of creditors, even if the identity of those creditors has, to a certain degree, changed, that is, become more international in character. Its austere and 'prudent' response to debt made its debt more attractive and thus more subject to investor scrutiny and sentiment. If anything, it now has less, not more, sovereign independence with regard to its policy choices. Second, these developments have only further undermined an important condition for creditworthiness: that the interests of creditors are represented in the formal structures of representative government. Despite BEE, this is still very much not the case in South Africa. We submit that, more than any other factor, it is this that explains the continued lack of credibility of South Africa, that is, it is this inability to complete the representative circle that explains why South Africa is still deemed a relatively risky place in which to invest.

Conclusion

In this chapter I have provided an account for the ANC's decision to choose an elite compromise with the outgoing NP government and the old, mainly 'white' economic elite and, in line with this decision, to adopt an austere fiscal policy following liberation from apartheid. I have shown why this decision not only was misguided but also has backfired to monumental and dangerous proportions: besides constraining any subsequent policy decisions that might have been in the interests of economic transformation and the empowerment of the citizenry as a whole, despite making all the right moves in terms of the economic orthodoxy of the age, the South African state still lacks the credibility needed for relatively cheap debt servicing and economic transformation. This is because the elite compromise depended on forms of economic and political representation that not only reinforced rather than recalibrated existing power relations and forms of domination, but also disabled South Africa from gaining the levels of creditworthiness that ought to have been the result of constituting representative democracy. Thus the accommodation by the new political elite of the old economic elite was, despite the discourses and promises of the age, the recipe for stagnation and continued domination rather than growth and empowerment of all for two reasons. First, the economic elite do not have strict veto power over political decision-making, and thus international investors still deem South Africa a risky place in which to invest. Second, it is not in the short-term interests of the economic elite to push for a change in these cosy relations of power with the new political elite.

Of course, the folly of these decisions and, ultimately, the faith in elite compromise are partly explained by the lack of experience in government and training in economics at the helm of the ANC in the early 1990s, which required an over-reliance on IMF and World Bank experts.[42] The consequence of this over-reliance on the experts, moreover, was not helped by the fact that not only were the orthodox economic arguments swallowed hook, line and sinker, but also the orthodox arguments regarding the causal relationship amongst representative democracy, public debt and state credibility are fundamentally flawed, at least in the case of South Africa, but potentially in all contexts. State credibility is best defined as the perceived likelihood that a current or future government will honour debt contracts.[43] Increased state credibility is associated with a significant drop in the premia states have to pay to service their debts; in other words, as credibility increases, so the cost to a state of its debt decreases.

The received opinion on public debt and state credibility is that representative democracies are much better suited to public borrowing than autocracies or other forms of political regime because they display greater commitment to debt repayment, or, in other words, are less likely to default on debt.[44] This is the case, various economists and political scientists have argued, for a number of possible reasons. (1) In democracies, as long as the state borrows from its citizens, 'there is no divergence of interest between borrower and lenders, for the two are one and the same.[45] (2) Limited or 'Mixed' government creates the constitutional checks and balances necessary to ensure commitment.[46] (3) Representative democracies normally delegate management of government debt to an independent agency, like a central bank, which increases commitment by making it more costly for a government to default on its debts: since government revenue is channelled through the bank, any decision to default would quickly lead to a halt in payments from bank to government.[47] (4) Credible commitment in democracies is the result of the concomitant growth and significance of parties and party government, which generate compromises and concessions that lead to moderate policies and thus a reduction in the possibility for default.[48]

---

[42] Terreblanche, *Lost*, provides much evidence for this over reliance.

[43] Stasavage, *Public Debt*, p. 23.

[44] Macdonald, *Free Nation Deep in Debt*, p. 6.

[45] Macdonald, *Free Nation Deep in Debt*, p. 7.

[46] C. de Montesquieu, *The Spirit of the Laws* (Cambridge: Cambridge University Press, 1989 [1748]); A. Hamilton, J. Madison and J. Jay, *The Federalist*, ed. T. Ball (Cambridge: Cambridge University Press, 2003 [1787]); North and Weingast, 'Constitutions and Commitment'.

[47] B. Weingast, 'The Political Foundations of Limited Government: Parliament and Sovereign Debt in 17th and 18th Century England', in *Frontiers of the New Institutional Economics*, ed. J. Drobak and J. Nye (London: Harcourt Brace, 1997), pp. 213–246.

[48] E. E. Schattschneider, *Party Government* (New York: Farrar and Rinehart, 1942).

(5) Representative democracies support the free movement of capital and are therefore also more wary of taxing it heavily to avoid capital flight. This may be equally true with regard to taxes on capital and for default, which may be seen as one-off tax on holders of government bonds.[49] In sum, the orthodox argument holds that representative democracy is a necessary (and in some instances even a sufficient) condition for credibility, that is, that its institution reduces uncertainty and thus increases the value of a state's bonds, which means it becomes less expensive for a government to finance its activities.

Our evidence as regards the recent history of South Africa casts doubt on all of these arguments. The first argument given by Macdonald seems to rest on a naïve notion of democracy because even if all creditors were citizens, in representative democracies it is highly unlikely that there will be *no* divergence of interest between borrowers and lenders, or between rulers and ruled. In any case, this assumption clearly does not fit in the case of South Africa. Second, the case of South Africa makes it clear that constituting representative democracy, including all the necessary checks and balances, is not sufficient to ensure credibility. South Africa remains a risky place in which to invest, despite its consolidation of representative democracy and adoption of prudent fiscal management, even beyond that expected by the IMF. Nor do the third and fifth reasons hold much water under South African conditions, for while, similar to other representative democracies, the South African government does delegate some of its fiscal management to its central bank it still maintains exchange control and therefore bucks the alleged trend that representative democracies support capital mobility. Finally, the fourth reason depends upon a strict condition that does not obtain in all representative democracies and is clearly not the case in South Africa – that there must be conflict over multiple issues and the dividing lines in each conflict do not coincide. As I have shown in this book, the dividing lines in South African society are still very much determined by the coincidence of racial divisions and those generated by poverty, unemployment and inequality.

Rather, the more likely reason that representative democracies normally bring about an increase in a state's credibility is that they have tended to provide the representatives of the creditor class with a veto point in parliament. This is not the case yet in South Africa and so it lacks credibility, worsened by the associated macroeconomic straitjacket that disallows for meaningful

---

[49] Stasavage, *Public Debt*, p. 23; C. Lindblom, 'The Market as Prison', *Journal of Politics*, 44.2 (1982), pp. 324–326.

intervention to counter the effects of the cleavages generated by centuries of racial domination and political and economic exclusion. International creditor interests are represented (through identification) by an economic elite that does not enjoy formal representation in parliament and therefore both international and national creditors do not control a veto point. Thus the case of South Africa supports this broader theoretical claim regarding representative democracies: that what really matters is not so much the instantiation of representative democracy *per se*, but that representative democracy normally provides a relevant veto point for the creditor class. Whether it supports the strong version of the claim – that the necessary condition for a state's credibility is the formal, political representation of its national creditors, irrespective of the exact form of its regime – is up for debate. This more demanding theoretical claim could only properly be substantiated by means of a comparison of various examples of public debt management, representation and state credibility, which I must pass on here.[50]

What I can say, though, is that this argument regarding representative democracy, public debt and state credibility in South Africa highlights the importance of understanding the dynamics of public debt for an understanding of representation and *vice versa*. All governments need creditors, even under conditions of austerity, and so creditors are in a privileged position as regards the formation of fiscal policy. They retain the power to discipline government by dint of the fact that the state cannot function without their credit. If their interests are accorded formal, political representation, they control a veto point; if not, their country will be deemed less creditworthy than those that do, which in itself provides a strong incentive for the formal political representation of their interests. This suggests that at the very least the orthodox argument must be augmented and that the weakest form of my argument here holds, at least in the case of South Africa: that both representative democracy and the formal, political representation of a state's national creditors together constitute necessary conditions for credibility. Within modern representative democracies, as in South Africa, the clamour is no longer 'no taxation without representation';

---

[50] But for comparative support, especially from seventeenth and eighteenth century Holland and the UK, see North and Weingast, 'Constitutions and Commitment'; Weingast, 'The Political Foundations of Limited Government', in the context of Stasavage, *Public Debt*, pp. 5–6, not forgetting that the governments of both Holland and the United Kingdom for most of the seventeenth and eighteenth century were far from what, much later, became known as 'representative democracies', in fact the term had yet to be coined – see B. Manin, *The Principles of Representative Government* (Cambridge: Cambridge University Press, 1997); and J. Dunn, *Setting the People Free: The Story of Democracy* (London: Atlantic Books, 2005). In other words, whether or not they could borrow cheaply had nothing to do with their status or otherwise as 'representative democracies'.

rather the reality is 'no credit without representation'. Not taking this and its consequences seriously enough and not working out how best to square this reality with the dire need to overcome South Africa's long legacy of racial oppression and devastatingly high levels of inequality, unemployment and poverty have been the most serious indictment of the ANC in government.

Conclusion

Overcoming South Africans' Lack of Freedom

If freedom is conceived of in realistic, substantive and practically meaningful terms, as 'freedom as power through political representation', we have no option but to conclude that South Africans are not yet free, or so I argue in this book. South Africans lack power across a whole range of interrelated social, economic and political domains and this lack of power translates into living under at least one of four possible states of domination. The proximate cause for this deleterious state of affairs, I submit, was the elite compromise reached during the transition to democracy – still strongly maintained today – that generated forms of economic and political representation that fail to empower and thus free the citizens of South Africa. This is the case because the elite compromise reified rather than enabled the transformation of power relations that had been generated under and inherited from colonial and apartheid regimes and conditions, hardly good bases for real modern freedom. In other words, Nelson Mandela was right to warn his fellow citizens that mere political liberation would not necessarily and easily bring real freedom. Not only is the journey to the latter a long and difficult one, requiring constant vigilance, courage and active critique, but also it depends upon having the process of liberation itself generate the right institutions for the achievement and maintenance of freedom as power. Democratic South Africa did not enjoy this kind of auspicious institutional birth, notwithstanding its compliance with all of the contemporary global strictures regarding the institutional configuration of constitutional democracy. As a result, I argue, even if the requisite levels of vigilance, activism, courage and critique abound, they often amount to yelling against the wind or the generation of false hope.

More exactly, as developed in Chapter 1, I argue that freedom is relative to an individual's power to: (a) get what she wants, to act or be as she would choose in the absence of either internal or external obstacles or both; (b) determine the government of her political association; (c) develop and exercise her powers and capacities self-reflectively within and against existing norms, expectations and power relations; and (d) determine her social and economic environment via meaningful control over her economic and political representatives. In other words, power is integral to freedom across most of the domains that are significant for individual existence within complex, modern polities.[1] As supported by empirical evidence on quality-of-life statistics for South Africa and the nature of the various forms of economic and political representation that still prevail therein, I argued more specifically that South Africans lack freedom across all of these dimensions or at least some, and this translates into living within one or more states of domination. I argued, in short, that freedom is power through representation across various domains and that, given that South Africa has failed to instantiate the relevant forms of representation, South Africans continue to lack freedom to a debilitating degree. In other words, freedom is a matter of degree; and, although South Africans are freer than they were under apartheid, they are a lot less free than they might otherwise have been had their representatives instantiated institutions that enabled freedom as power across all of these four dimensions of freedom as power and thus avoided or helped overcome various states of domination. The focus, ultimately, was on the following facts: that existing, skewed forms of economic and political representation reproduce the power and interests of elites rather than generate economic opportunity and political power for all; that South Africa's electoral system implements the idea of proportional representation so literally that it undermines rather than instantiates meaningful representation and thus removes any meaningful political agency from ordinary citizens; and that existing macroeconomic policy fails to address the dire conditions of poverty, inequality, unemployment, inadequate education and thus the provision of freedom as power for all South Africans.

The anatomy of contemporary South Africa should by now have removed all doubt in the mind of the reader that Mandela is right to claim that South Africans are not yet free. Mandela is wrong, however, if by going on to maintain that freedom in South Africa depends on each of us living our lives 'in a way that respects and enhances the freedom of others' he means that we all have a *duty* (Christian or otherwise) to actively aid others in the attainment of their freedom, and we will only be free if we act in accordance with this alleged duty or obligation. This laudable notion is not just unrealistic, especially under modern conditions; it does not tell the complete story. Our being free *does* depend on the freedom of others, but not in the sense Mandela suggests. South Africans, as with

---

[1] For the full theoretical defence of this point, see L. Hamilton, *Freedom Is Power: Liberty Through Political Representation* (Cambridge: Cambridge University Press, 2014).

citizens all over the globe, live interdependent lives, and it is this unavoidable interdependence that makes our individual degree of freedom integral to that of every other citizen and *vice versa*. The causally significant relation between very high levels of poverty, inequality, unemployment and violent crime, racial mistrust, fear and anxiety coupled with the fact that a significant portion of the population is not organized for collective action, civil disobedience or resistance because of the very high levels of unemployment, which highlights not only this interdependence but also the severity of the situation in South Africa. But it does not follow from the fact that every citizen's degree of freedom is dependent on the degree of freedom of every other citizen that the resolution is to be found uniquely in the moral rectitude or civic duty or civil disobedience of citizens. I argue that those thinkers who emphasize active resistance alone as the panacea for the kinds of problems found within South Africa make two related errors. First, their pleas for creative interventions by ordinary citizens (as civil society activists or otherwise) assume levels of moral and political duty and commitment that are only true of a very small number of activists. The rest of the population do not have either the time and means or inclination to fight for justice and freedom every step of the way. Second, they miss the all-important fact that most protests are single-issue claims that reflect a lack of voice, that is, representation, amongst those involved in the protest in question. Infrequently do protests constitute demands for real rebellion or revolutionary change or complete structural reform, though under extant conditions of representation in South Africa, as protest numbers mushroom along with the extent to which they use violence to have their claims heard, it is not completely out of the question to suppose that repeated frustration at not being listened to could begin to take on revolutionary proportions.

The lack of respect for existing laws and the increasingly frequent turn to extra-legal means of having one's needs and interests recognized are not however a recipe for social, economic and political instantiation of freedom as power. It is an expression of the extreme lack of power experienced by most of South Africa's population. To understand this requires us to reformulate what Mandela may have meant when he said that freedom in South Africa depends on each of us living our lives 'in a way that respects and enhances the freedom of others'.

First, we have to expand it beyond its merely moral basis into a strict coercively enforceable legal sanction: that the desire and capacity to respect the law and the freedom of others depend not only on the law (and its enforcement) but also on the extent to which any society is able to provide for the vital and agency needs of its citizenry and thus enable sufficient power for the them to act freely. In other words, the individual desire or capacity to respect the law and respect and enhance the freedom of others do not ultimately depend upon individual moral rectitude or response to a 'universal' duty or obligation to do so, but on each citizen's power to act as they would otherwise do, resist the norms of their society and control their economic and political environment through their representatives. Particularly as regards resistance, Flathman puts this insight well: 'Having resisted and partly freed themselves from the received, the conventional, and the authoritative, they are themselves free in a distinctive sense and their feeling, thinking and acting sometimes enlarges and enhances the freedom of others'.[2] In other words, as has also been argued by the likes of Montaigne, Marx, Nietzsche, Foucault, Fanon and Hampshire, if we have any obligation regarding freedom it is first and foremost to free ourselves: '[A] person's cultivation of her own individuality is a good, not a duty owed to others'.[3] The substance of conceptions of individuality and freedom will vary from person to person, so if there is anything that we owe others it is to encourage their cultivation of their own individualities and 'free-spiritedness' and to respect their freedom to pursues these goods as long as doing so does not hinder others in their achievement and maintenance of their freedom and individuality. The constant enactment of our freedom therefore depends upon certain political conditions that enable both the individual ability constantly to assess the norms and laws of our society and respect for the freedom of other members of our society to be involved in the same project of individual action and judgement.

Second, once this is understood it becomes possible to see that it is not just in the interest of the powerless that their power be enhanced, but also the interest of the powerful and seemingly free. To them too we can say that it is in your interest to respect, encourage and enhance the freedom of others, that is, to empower them, since the more freedom as power they have, the more likely they are to respect your power and freedom. This provides the powerful elites with a much greater incentive to enable the freedom of the less powerful than an argument based on moral injunction or civic virtue alone. The veiled, credible threat that underpins it, and that South Africans of all classes feel every day, is a much greater spur to action than either the motivating forces of moral imperative or solidarity. The veiled, credible threat is, of course, the following: if our freedom as power is not enabled we will not be able to respect the freedom

---

[2] R. E. Flathman, *Freedom and Its Conditions: Discipline, Autonomy and Resistance* (London: Routledge, 2003), p. 169.

[3] Flathman, *Freedom and Its Conditions*, p. 155.

and power of others in general and the legal order of South Africa, in particular. In other words, the force of real revolution, as conceived here, is not the result of cumulative effects of disjointed rebellions, but on an organized and credible threat that we – ordinary South African citizens – will threaten the very survival of the post-apartheid political order for which so many lost their lives and that, despite its shortcomings, is still so prized today. The very legal edifice upon which the elite compromise depends will itself be jeopardized. Put in these terms, and if real and credible, the elites will quickly come to see that they need to rearrange the economic and political order *in order* to safeguard *their own* most basic interests. This way, the needs and interests of the majority that lack freedom as power through representation quickly become if not equivalent to then at least safeguarded by the same recalibration of existing economic and political institutions and forms or representation. So, we might reformulate Mandela as follows: to be free is to live in a society in which our obedience to the law gives us the power to do what we want and reflect critically on the norms of our society and act on the power we must have over our economic and political environment and representatives; and when we are not provided with these conditions our obedience to the law falls away entirely.

That real freedom depends upon citizens' mounting credible threats to the *ultima ratio* of the polity's stability, that is, the state's monopoly of legitimate violence, is a logical extension of this book's main argument. As I put it in Chapter 1, in South Africa it is not so much a case of 'revolution suspended'[4] as 'revolution still pending'. Or, to be more exact, it is the *threat* of revolution that may be necessary for real freedom to obtain in South Africa. In other words, freedom as power in South Africa depends upon the recalibration of institutional power relations, which, short of revolution itself, can only be brought about by the *credible threat* of revolution, especially given the elite pacted conditions that exist in South Africa. Moreover, as is instantiated by the argument I developed in Chapter 4 regarding the relationship between a state's creditors, the existing forms of political representation and the very credibility of the state itself, this recalibration of power relations is best understood in terms of class or group power relations and forms of representation. In general within capitalist representative democracies the power of the creditor class, or at least the power of their representatives, far outweighs that of any other class or group, which is a direct result of the fact that under conditions of global capitalism states have

---

[4]   A. Habib, *South Africa's Suspended Revolution: Hopes and Prospects* (Johannesburg: Wits University Press, 2013).

a constant need for affordable credit as has been made clearly evident in the aftermath of the recent global credit crisis. The management of public debt in South Africa during and following its period of negotiated transition from apartheid has only reinforced the skewed power relations that exist between the creditor class and the rest of the polity and exacerbated their effects. Thus the mainstream economic orthodoxy coupled with the structure of these power relations creates a condition of domination that severely affects the freedom of the poor and unemployed in South Africa, and also the wealthy, for the reasons discussed in Chapter 2 – even the freedom of the most wealthy are affected by the lack of freedom of the rest of the polity.

It is clear, moreover, that the elites around the negotiating table did not feel any severe pressure to look around them – potentially outside the western orthodoxy of the time – and propose or experiment with different ideas. There were in fact a number of differing models to hand, some very obviously being experienced and some more theoretical suggestions in very widely disseminated political economic literature. The folly of the new South African government's choice is highlighted by the experience of at least eight rapidly growing Asian economies between 1960 and 1980, all of whom achieved their rapid growth on the back of a significant narrowing of inequality, with regard in particular to land ownership and income distribution.[5] Moreover, exactly when the new political elites in South Africa were making their ill-fated decision, these East Asian examples were the subject of a range of well-publicised studies, as was a similar study of at least nine OECD countries and two worldwide studies of 67 and 70 different countries, respectively, all showing a robust causal relationship between greater equity and growth and, conversely, that wider income and ownership differentials are associated with slower growth. All show, furthermore, that the direction of causality was from equality to growth. Moreover, the second of the larger studies noted above, carried out by Alesina and Perotti, found that investment tended to be higher in countries with narrower income differences and that this was because income differences reduced investment by contributing to political instability.[6]

If this latter finding is coupled with my argument regarding creditor representation, the following message rings loud for South Africa. Had

---

[5] N. Birdsall, D. Ross and R. Sabot, 'Inequality and Growth Reconsidered – Lessons from East Asia', *World Bank Economic Review*, 9.3 (1995), pp. 477–508; World Bank, *The East Asian Miracle* (Oxford: Oxford University Press, 1993).

[6] T. Persson and G. Tabellini, 'Is Inequality Harmful for Growth? Theory and Evidence', *American Economic Review*, 84.3 (1994), pp. 600–621; see also various studies cited in R. G. Wilkinson, *Unhealthy Societies: The Afflictions of Inequality* (London: Routledge, 1996), p. 225.

South Africa's economic and political leaders bothered to take notice of these experiences and findings (or if they did know about them then at least take them seriously), South Africa might have learnt a lot from them and undertaken their strategy of generating growth, employment and investment in exactly the opposite way to the one they chose: to redistribute wealth and opportunity first and then watch as growth and investment followed. Instead, as I have argued in this book, the decision regarding the management of public debt was undertaken as a consequence of a desire to attain two goals – autonomy from national capital and greater independence from international financial institutions – both of which have backfired.

From the outset therefore the elite compromise and associated macroeconomic decisions, more than any others, have entrenched inherited and existing forms of domination and thus made the majority of South Africans less rather than more free, in other words, less free than they could have been had different choices been made. Not only do the formal forms of representation not enable South Africans to express their needs and interests and ensure that their representatives act to satisfy them, but also the existing informal kinds of representation effectively maintain the status quo of high levels of poverty and inequality. Representation, participation and control are therefore important not only because they enable power within these domains of freedom but also because they enable individuals to empower themselves through the meaningful determination of their needs. Moreover, there is now little doubt that the extent of poverty, unemployment and inequality in South Africa, as outlined in Chapter 2, is a direct result of the adoption of these two forms of representation and the associated decisions that followed, for example, the economic policy decision in 1996 to substitute a strongly redistributivist and interventionist Reconstruction and Development Programme (RDP) for the more fiscally conservative and monetarist policy of Growth, Employment and Redistribution (GEAR).[7] It follows therefore that the various domains of freedom as power discussed in this book are not only inter-related but also that freedom from poverty and inequality depends, at least in part, on the power to control the economic and political environment via meaningful control over one's political representatives. Freedom in South Africa, as elsewhere, therefore depends on the relatively equal power of influence that all South African citizens wield over macro-political and macroeconomic decisions via meaningful control over their political representatives. This is not possible under prevailing economic and political conditions and orthodoxies, an

---

[7]   T. Lodge, *Politics in South Africa: From Mandela to Mbeki* (Cape Town: David Philip, 2002), p. 26.

electoral system that privileges the interest of parties above the needs of citizens and a debt management system that puts economic stability and the interests of creditors before redistribution and empowerment.

What cannot be avoided, however, in all of this, is the need to conceive of alternative institutions to achieve and maintain freedom as power and to think about how our choice regarding them can be carried out and done so legitimately. It is one thing discussing electoral reform, for example, but it is quite another coming to a decision regarding how best to proceed and then generate the mechanisms and the will to implement the decision. Talk is easy: for example, currently in South Africa it is not just a few opposition parties – in particular the DA – who talk about the need for electoral reform but also now even the ANC is calling for it.[8] However, as I have noted above, the chance of any success regarding institutional choice will depend upon real and credible threats from the populous at large. Moreover, unlike the various calls from different political parties, my suggestions regarding electoral reform are only one component of a series of suggestions regarding institutional reform and implementation to avoid the terror of real revolution. It is worth reiterating that real revolution – not something as vacuous and meaningless as the ANC's doctrine of 'national democratic revolution' – is a real possibility, unless institutional conditions undergo radical recalibration, and that all will be worse off were it not to be avoided. My proposals for far-reaching institutional change for South Africa's electoral democracy are aimed at enhancing political agency and legitimacy. Moreover, some of them may actually work better without election but through sortition, deliberation, contestation, direct plebiscite and so on.

As I have argued throughout, the control over the determination of one's needs is vital for freedom, for without it citizens easily become mere pawns in larger games in which other citizens or citizen groups effectively determine the needs and desires of less-powerful citizens as they pursue their own goals within existing power relations. Freedom as power depends upon what I call here and elsewhere the 'power to determine needs': the power to identify, express and evaluate my needs, interests and their formative practices and institutions.[9] However, as was argued in Chapter 3, this kind of direct control over need determination is unrealistic and even undesirable. Representation is unavoidable and desirable as it frees us up from having to satisfy all of our own needs all of the time. Thus representative institutions are directly linked to the avoidance of

[8] N. Marrian, 'Mashatile Wants Constituencies for MPs', *Business Day*, 25 July 2013, p. 3.
[9] L. Hamilton, *The Political Philosophy of Needs* (Cambridge: Cambridge University Press, 2003); and Hamilton, *Freedom Is Power*.

what I call, following Foucault, states of domination, but departing from him by combining the language of needs and institutions. The degree to which one lives in a state of domination, I argued, depends upon the extent and kind of power one has to determine one's needs. States of domination of this kind can take a number of different forms:

a)   The existing power relations may persistently mislead me and members of my groups in our attempts to *identify* our needs, either through direct coercion (leading us to deny our needs) or intentional manipulation ('persuading' us, say, that another group's needs are ours) or as a result of fixed, traditional norms and practices, a good example of which is patriarchy and the continued subordination of women.

b)   I may live under a regime that does not give me and other members of my group or groups the power to *express* our needs, for example, as a black person within apartheid South Africa, where political rights were deemed the privileges of whites alone and the institutional means through which, as a black person, I might have expressed my needs and interests had been removed (or, more exactly, never properly instantiated and then removed).

c)   I live in a polity that disallows meaningful *evaluation* of needs and interests; a form of regime that may provide me and other members of my groups with the formal means and freedoms to identify our needs and even express them without fear of prejudice or harm – it may even seek much of its legitimacy from exactly these two freedoms – but in real, specifically economic, terms is based upon the kinds of practices and institutions that either disallow the evaluation of needs and interests or fail to provide the institutions through which this would be achieved, such as a polity founded on pre-political natural or human rights coupled with an economy in which *only* revealed preferences for consumer goods are deemed valuable. Good, but not unique, examples of this are free-market-dominated polities, for instance, the United States of America. Moreover, the worst manifestations of these problems are felt most acutely in less wealthy and more unequal societies such as South Africa and Angola.

The only answer then is the creation and defence of political institutions whose main function is to identify and overcome states of domination and generate freedom as power for all citizens and groups in society. Moreover, given the existing power relations, the only way that rulers and ruled are both together going to be able to see that these kinds of institutions are necessary is if the alternative of potentially highly destructive revolution to the existing stable order becomes a real and credible threat and we remain realistic about the need for partisan institutions, conflicting groups and interests and the kinds of antagonistic politics that follow. To that end then, I end this book by proposing a few institutions in this realistic spirit, institutions that I argue respond directly to the lack of freedom as power for all South Africans.

The kinds of political institutions that would be necessary for citizens to have meaningful control over their needs and their representatives would have to give them both the positive power to legislate and the negative power to repeal legislation, whilst also providing their representatives with the freedom to legislate. This seemingly paradoxical requirement is possible if we take both the need for representation and participation seriously and thus institutionalize changes at the local, legislative and constitutional levels. For power really to be returned to the people and thus for freedom to prevail in South Africa a number of changes have to be effected. The first four pertain to specific changes that could, in effect, be carried out under the existing macro-political structure. The last four are proposed changes to the macro-political structure itself. However, I see no reason why all eight could not be established by the existing government in South Africa, though whether the ANC-led alliance have the will, courage and interest in doing so is of course another matter entirely. The second group of four institutional arrangements in particular would both empower citizens to participate periodically in the determination of their needs and their constitution and give them a power of veto or repeal over legislation and a power of recall or impeachment of existing representatives.

a) Sovereignty must be returned to parliament.
b) Real redistribution of wealth and power amongst the various groups that make up 'the people' must be carried out.
c) South Africa's electoral system must be completely reorganized to enable real and meaningful competition to represent the various individuals and groups that constitute the South African polity, a good model being a mixture of proportional representation and constituency-based first-post-systems, along the lines adopted by Ireland and Germany, amongst others.
d) Macroeconomic policy must be introduced that is specifically targeted towards meeting people's needs and overcoming domination (and thus empowering) all South Africans.
e) *District Assemblies* – local physical sites with five main functions: (i) to enable the articulation and evaluation of needs and interests, the substantive outcome of which would then be transferred by the district's counselor to the national assembly for further debate and, ultimately, legislation; (ii) to

make available to citizens full accounts of all the legislative activity and results emanating from the national assembly; (iii) to provide a forum for the presentation of amendments to existing legislation; (iv) to vote on proposals coming from other assemblies; and (v) to select counselors for the revitalized consiliar system. The determination of the exact geography (and thus borders) of these sites would be heavily contested in the South African case, but I see no reason why this ought to be a constraint on implementation.[10] Constituency borders under most forms of political representation and electoral system constitute a matter of dispute and contestation, but then so do most things in politics. At least one guiding principle must be kept to the fore: each district should always, at least as far as is possible, incorporate as diverse a group of the national population as possible, especially as regards social and economic power relations – the full spectrum of conditions, needs and interests must be incorporated.

f)   *A Revitalized Consiliar System*: (i) would rest on the network of district assemblies; (ii) each district assembly would select one counselor for a two-year period, who would be responsible for providing counsel to the representatives in the national assembly regarding the *local* needs and interests of the citizenry and existing institutional configurations and their links to states of domination – that is, what changes may be required to better satisfy needs and interests and diminish the possibility for states of domination in the local area in question; (iii) the main role of the counselors is therefore biased towards the defence of the interests of the various groups or classes of citizenry within the district in question, whose needs and interests would surface within district assemblies, and thus the powers and responsibilities of district counselors would not only be much greater than those of councillors within existing forms of local government, but also in order for them to carry out these functions, their independence from national representatives, political parties and social and economic elites would have to be procedurally safeguarded within the constitution. I say 'select' and not 'elect' counselors as, given the formal and merely procedural function of counselors in this

---

[10] *Cf.* the proposals that emerged from the Electoral Task Team, 'Report of the Electoral Task Team' [online] (January 2003), Available from: http://www.unisa.ac.za/news/wp-content/uploads/2013/04/Van-Zyl-Slabbert-Commission-on-Electoral-Reform-Report-2003.pdf [accessed 20 September 2013]. This report has been left to gather dust by parliament with no effect on South Africa's electoral system, I maintain, mainly because it provided two potential routes for parliament, one of which was the maintenance of the status quo, which parliament obviously ultimately chose. It qualified its more radical proposal for electoral reform based upon the claim that any form of constituency-based electoral system would create too much political division and conflict in South Africa, something to be avoided at all cost. The time has come, I argue, to be bolder and face the unavoidable reality of discord in politics.

proposal, their selection could be undertaken by election or sortition (lottery). I favour the latter as local, district assemblies are prone to fall prey to local factions and interests that may work against the point of this form of local participation; in other words, each counselor must literally advise – give counsel to – the national assembly on the conditions, needs and interests of those she or he represents. Were the counselors to be too easily captured by social and economic elites or always come from these elites – as is the case in most national assemblies within existing representative democracies – they would not help in the necessary process of countering domination: it would be much easier for them to defend elite interests rather than those of any other group or class. Of course, checks and balances and forms of accountability and transparency could be included to ensure that they do carry forward the needs and interests as articulated and determined in the district assemblies, but, given that the district assemblies will be constituted by normal citizens leading busy personal and commercial lives, even these kinds of institutional checks and balances may not ensure that counselors conform to their station, as citizens are likely not to have the time properly to monitor counselors 'all the way up the political chain of command'.[11]

g) *Updated Tribune of the Plebs*: (i) a partisan, separate and independent institution of legislation for the exclusive membership of representatives of otherwise dominated groups and classes in society, whose membership could be made exclusively for representatives from this class either by a net household worth ceiling or by associated measures, enabling those with the least economic power in any polity both to propose and to repeal (or veto) legislation and impeach national representatives, but with strict and low per annum limits on the number of times this could be carried out – here too the selection of representatives could, by means of election or sortition, again favour the latter, for similar reasons to those stated above;[12] and (ii) a

---

[11] For more on district assemblies and an explanation of my adoption of the term and institution of 'counselor' from Ancient Rome (as opposed to the more normal modern English term and institution of 'councillor'), see L. Hamilton, 'Human Needs and Political Judgment' in *New Waves in Political Philosophy*, ed. B. de Bruin and C. Zurn (London: Palgrave, 2008), pp. 40–62. The revised account of 'district assemblies' submitted here, especially (ii) – (iv) above, also draws from Condorcet's notion of 'primary assemblies'. For more on these and how they therefore become sites for both the positive and negative powers of sovereignty (legislation and repeal), see N. Urbinati, *Representative Democracy: Principles and Genealogy* (Chicago: Chicago University Press, 2008), pp. 207–213.

[12] As expressed, for example, in Machiavelli's defence of the Roman Tribune of the Plebs in his *Discourses*, recently updated by J. P. McCormick in his *Machiavellian Democracy* (Cambridge: Cambridge University Press, 2011), pp. 184–187 and *passim*, but here with more emphasis on legislative proposition and repeal than on mere veto power or power of impeachment against representatives.

partisan, separate and independent electoral procedure by means of which the least powerful groups or classes in society would have exclusive rights to elect at least one quarter of national representatives for the national assembly, alongside the normal, open party-dominated processes of electing representatives within most existing representative democracies. This second component of the updated tribune of the plebs is intended to offset the potentially merely reactive character of the first and to withstand the very real possibility that the national assembly or assemblies would hamstring a plebeian chamber of this kind by various means, such as using up its power of veto of one piece of legislation per annum by first proposing mock legislation that it knows will be vetoed and then, once the per annum quota of veto has been used up, going ahead with anti-plebeian legislation about which the tribune could then do nothing.[13]

h) *Constitutional Revision and Safeguard*: (i) a decennial plebiscite, following a month-long carnival of citizenship – a public holiday – in which all citizens would have equal formal freedom and power to assess existing social, economic and political institutional matrices and their affects on the determination and satisfaction of vital and agency needs[14]; (ii) a right of constitutional revision that would have to be procedurally safeguarded, that is, a right of any citizen at any point to propose the assessment and possible revision of a component of the constitution, which in Condorcet, as in Jefferson and Paine, is based on two important arguments, namely, *antityranny*, that is, shielding present and future generations from the unchecked power of past generations, and *fallibility*, that is, that reason is prone to error and subject to change over time and thus it is important to presume the need for permanent revision to the constitution[15]; and (iii) *procedural* safeguards giving priority to the satisfaction of *vital* needs, safeguarding counselors from manipulation, coercion and corruption, ensuring the administration of district assemblies and the partisan institutions, and enabling constitutional revision.[16]

Together these four main institutional changes would provide sufficient power, class antagonism and institutional checks and balances to generate and safeguard

---

[13] For these and other criticisms and concerns with McCormick's proposal, see the symposium on his book in *The Good Society*, 20.2 (2011), and his responses in 20.3.

[14] L. Hamilton, "'(I've Never Met) a Nice South African": Virtuous Citizenship and Popular Sovereignty', *Theoria*, Issue 119, 56.2 (June 2009), pp. 57–80.

[15] Urbinati, *Representative Democracy*, 184–187.

[16] This is based upon an important distinction between the procedural components of a constitution, such as counselor independence, and the more substantive components, such as which existing needs and rights, besides vital needs, are and ought to have priority.

freedom as power for all individuals and groups in South Africa, or at least ensure against one powerful group usurping the freedom as power of all the citizens and groups that constitute the South African polity. As the four dimensions of freedom as power highlight, freedom is not only to do with power in the sense of my ability to carry out my intended actions, it is also to do with power in the sense of citizen and societal group control over who rules and how they rule, in other words, over political representatives. Real modern freedom is not captured by means of either 'private' freedom or 'political' freedom. The former generates the unhelpful allergic reaction to political regulation found in the thought and practice of free market ideologues and most libertarian liberals and the latter ignores the fact that much everyday modern freedom is determined by the various social, political and economic groups, practices, institutions and forms of representation that enable our power to satisfy our needs and overcome states of domination. Freedom as power through political representation, in the form defended here, brings all these directly to the fore in an account of the social, economic and political conditions for freedom of action.

All of the above would, of course, be aided by the existence of competent, courageous, responsible and persuasive leaders and a restructuring of the ANC-led ruling alliance; however, conversely too, good leadership and judgement would also be an important consequence of these institutional changes. In politics, the causal relationship between the political virtue of leaders and the institutional arrangements within which they make their decisions is always complex and bidirectional, but that should be no reason for political conservatism. Although good habits and sentiments are necessary for good judgement, good institutions are more likely to generate the necessary habits than habits on their own are to generate the necessary good institutions.

In sum, then, I have defended the idea that South Africans lack freedom for reasons slightly different from the ones suggested by Mandela, but in doing so I maintain that his general claim is a valid one. In contrast to Mandela's emphasis on moral duty, if we follow my argument regarding freedom is power through to its logical conclusion in the case of South Africa, it becomes unambiguously clear to any realistic observer that it is not our sense of duty to the freedom of others that will enable South Africans to be free; rather, it is the realization that our own individual freedom depends upon the freedom of others in our society, and that therefore it is in each of our own individual interests to help secure the freedom as power of all members of our society. South Africans lack freedom and they will remain in this condition until all South Africans are empowered across the four dimensions of freedom outlined in this book. This will not depend on goodwill, charity or duty, or on the complete realization of existing political and civil liberties, though these may help, but on courageous leadership, distinct institutions of economic and political representation to the ones that currently obtain, active and sometimes disobedient citizenship, good macroeconomic policy formation and implementation and radical redistribution of wealth and opportunity.

Bibliography

Adams, P., *Odious Debts: Loose Lending, Corruption, and the Third World's Environmental Legacy*, Oxford: Earthscan Publications, 1991.

Afrobarometer, Afrobarometer Briefing Paper No. 68 (2009). Available from: http://www.afrobarometer.org/papers/AfrobriefNo68_21may09_newfinal.pdf [accessed 19 July 2010].

Alvaredo, F., Atkinson, A. B., Piketty, T. and Saez, E. *The World Top Incomes Database*. Available from: http://topincomes.g-mond.parisschoolofeconomics.eu/#Database [accessed 28 August 2013].

ANC, 'Challenges of the Current Situation', *Discussion Document* (18 May 1993).

——, The Freedom Charter (2011) [1955]. Available from: http://www.anc.org.za/show.php?id=72 [accessed 30 July 2013].

Ankersmit, F. R., *Aesthetic Politics: Political Philosophy Beyond Fact and Value*, Stanford: Stanford University Press, 1997.

——, *Political Representation*, Stanford: Stanford University Press, 2002.

Arendt, H., *On Violence*, London: Allen Lane, 1970.

——, 'Freedom and Politics', in D. Miller (ed.), *The Liberty Reader*, Edinburgh: Edinburgh University Press, 2006 [1960].

Armstrong, P., Lekezwa, B. and Siebrits, K., 'Poverty in South Africa: A Profile Based on Recent Household Surveys', University of Stellenbosch (2008). Available from: http://www.ekon.sun.ac.za/wpapers/2008/wp042008/wp-04-2008.pdf [accessed 20 July 2010].

Arrow, K., *Social Choice and Individual Values*, New York: Wiley, 1951.

Barichievy, K., Piper, L. and Parker, B., 'Assessing "Participatory Governance" in Local Government: A Case-study of Two South African Cities', *Politeia*, 24 (3) (2005), 370–393.

Beinart, W., *Twentieth-Century South Africa*, Oxford: Oxford University Press, 2001.

Bentham, J., *Of Laws in General*, H. L. A. Hart (ed.), Oxford: Oxford University Press, 1970, ca. 1782.

Berlin, I., 'Two Concepts of Liberty', in *Four Essays on Liberty*, Oxford: Oxford University Press, 1996 [1969].

Birdsall, N., Ross, D. and Sabot, R., 'Inequality and Growth Reconsidered – Lessons from East Asia', *World Bank Economic Review*, 9 (3) (1995), 477–508.

Buchanan, J. M. and Tullock, G., *The Calculus of Consent: Logical Foundations of Constitutional Democracy*, Ann Arbor: University of Michigan Press, 1962.

Burke, E., 'Speech to the Electors of Bristol', in F. Canavan and E. J. Payne (eds), *Selected Works of Edmund Burke*, Indianapolis, IN: Liberty Fund, 1999 [1774], pp. 3–13.

Business Day, 'Police Not Backing Down on Violent Protests, Says Minister', *Business Day* (9 August 2012).

——, 'Ramaphosa May Have Fallen Victim to Political Manoeuvre', *Business Day* (25 October 2012). Available from: www.bdlive.co.za/blogs/politics/2012/10/25/ramaphosa-may-have-fallen-victim-to-a-political-manoeuvre [accessed 25 October 2012].

Butler, A., 'Black Economic Empowerment Since 1994: Diverse Hopes and Differentially Fulfilled Aspirations', in I. Shapiro and K. Tebeau (eds), *After Apartheid: Reinventing South Africa?*, Charlottesville: University of Virginia Press, 2011.

——, *The Idea of the ANC*, Johannesburg: Jacana, 2012.

Calitz, E., Du Plessis, S. and Siebrits, K., 'An Alternative Perspective on South Africa's Public Debt, 1962–1994', *South Journal of Economics*, Economic Society of South Africa, 79.2(2011), pp. 161–172.

Carter, I., *A Measure of Freedom*, Oxford: Oxford University Press, 1999.

Cohen, G. A., 'Capitalism, Freedom and the Proletariat', in D. Miller (ed.), *The Liberty Reader*, Edinburgh: Edinburgh University Press, 2006.

Condorcet, marquis de, *Foundations of Social Choice and Political Theory*, I. McLean and F. Hewitt (trans., eds), Aldershot: Edward Elgar, 1994.

Constitution of the Republic of South Africa, Eighth Edition, Cape Town: Juta & Co Ltd, 2009.

Dahl, R., *Democracy and Its Critics*, New Haven: Yale University Press, 1989.

Davenport, T. H. R. and Saunders, C., *South Africa: A Modern History*, London: MacMillan, 2000.

Davis, D., 'From the Freedom Charter to the Washington Consensus', in D. Everatt and V. Maphai (eds), *The Real State of the Nation: South Africa After the 1990s, Development Update (Special Edition)*, Johannesburg: Interfund, 4(3) (2003), 31–48.

De Kadt, R. and Simkins, C., 'The Political Economy of Pervasive Rent-seeking', *Thesis Eleven*, 115 (April 2013), 112–126.

De Klerk, F. W., 'We Astounded the World and Will Do So Again', *The Times* (13 February 2010), 24.

Dewey, J., *Problems of Men*, New York: Greenwood Press, 1968 [1946].

Donnelly, L., 'Welfare Could Be Gini in the Bottle', *Mail &Guardian* (10 May 2013).

Dryzek, J. S., *Deliberative Democracy and Beyond: Liberals, Critics, Contestations*, Oxford: Oxford University Press, 2000.

Du Plessis, L. M., 'A Background to Drafting the Chapter on Fundamental Rights', in B. de Villiers (ed.), *Birth of a Constitution*, Cape Town: Juta & Co, 1994, pp. 89–100.

Dubow, S., *The African National Congress*, Johannesburg: Jonathan Ball, 2000.

——, *The Struggle for Rights in South Africa*, Johannesburg: Jacana, 2010.

Dunn, J., 'The Politics of Representation and Good Government in Post-colonial Africa', in P. Chabal (ed.), *Political Domination in Africa*, Cambridge: Cambridge University Press, 1986.

——, *Western Political Theory in the Face of the Future*, Cambridge: Cambridge University Press (Canto Edition), 1993.

——, *Setting the People Free: The Story of Democracy*, London: Atlantic Books, 2005.

Electoral Task Team, 'Report of the Electoral Task Team' [online] (Cape Town: Electoral Task Team, January 2003), Available from: http://www.unisa.ac.za/news/wp-content/uploads/2013/04/Van-Zyl-Slabbert-Commission-on-Electoral-Reform-Report-2003.pdf [accessed 20 September 2013].

Eley, G., *Forging Democracy: The History of the Left in Europe, 1850–2000*, Oxford: Oxford University Press, 2002.

Fanon, F., *The Wretched of the Earth*, Paris: Présence Africaine, 1963.

——, *Black Skin, White Masks*, C. L. Markmann (trans.), London: Pluto Press, 1986.

Fedderke, J. W., De Kadt, R. H. J. and Luiz, J. M., 'Indicators of Political Liberty, Property Rights and Political Instability in South Africa: 1935–97', *International Review of Law and Economics*, 21 (2001), 103–134.

Fedderke, J. W. and Pillay, N., 'A Theoretically Defensible Measure of Risk: Using Financial Market Data from a Middle Income Context', Working Papers 64, Economic Research Southern Africa (2007).

Fehér, F., Heller, A. and Markus, G., *The Dictatorship Over Needs*, Oxford: Basil Blackwell, 1983.

Feinberg, J., 'Freedom and Liberty', in E. Craig (ed.), *Routledge Encyclopedia of Philosophy*, London: Routledge, 1998. Available from: http://www.rep.routledge.com/article/S026 [accessed 4 November 2009].

Flathman, R. E., *Freedom and Its Conditions: Discipline, Autonomy and Resistance*, London: Routledge, 2003.

Foucault, M., *Power/Knowledge: Selected Interviews and Other Writings, 1972–77*, Brighton: Harvester, 1980.

——, *Discipline and Punish*, New York: Penguin, 1991 [1975].

——, '"Omnes et Singulatim": Toward a Critique of Political Reason', in J. D. Faubion (ed.), *Essential Works, Vol 3: Power*, London: Penguin, 1997.

——, *The Will to Knowledge: The History of Sexuality, Vol 1*, R. Hurley (trans.), London: Penguin, 1998 [1976].

Freedom House, 1973–2013, *Freedom in the World*, Washington, DC: Freedom House. Available from: http://www.freedomhouse.org/report-types/freedom-world [accessed 2 October 2013].

Geuss, R., *The Idea of a Critical Theory*, Cambridge: Cambridge University Press, 1981.

——, *History and Illusion in Politics*, Cambridge: Cambridge University Press, 2001.

——, *Philosophy and Real Politics*, Princeton: Princeton University Press, 2008.

——, 'On the Very Idea of a Metaphysics of Right', in R. Geuss (ed.), Politics and the Imagination, Princeton: Princeton University Press, 2010.

Geuss, R. and Hamilton, L., 'Human Rights: A Very Bad Idea', interview of Raymond Geuss, *Theoria*, Issue 135, 60.2 (June 2013), pp. 83–103.

Gevisser, M., *Thabo Mbeki: The Dream Deferred*, Johannesburg: Jonathan Ball, 2007.

Green, P., 'Banking on Integrity', *Mail & Guardian*, (24 July 2009).

Gumede, W., *Thabo Mbeki and the Battle for the Soul of the ANC*, Cape Town: Zebra Press, 2005.

Gutmann, A. and Thompson, D., *Democracy and Disagreement*, Cambridge, MA: Harvard University Press, 1996.

Habermas, J., *The Theory of Communicative Action, 2 Vols*, T. McCarthy (trans.), Boston: Beacon Press, 1984/7.

——, *Between Facts and Norms: Contributions to a Discourse Theory of Law and Democracy*, Cambridge: Polity Press, 1996.

Habib, A., *South Africa's Suspended Revolution: Hopes and Prospects*, Johannesburg: Wits University Press, 2013.

Habib, A. and Padayachee, V., 'Economic Policy and Power in South Africa's Transition to Democracy', *World Development*, 28 (2) (2000), 245–263.

Hamilton, L., *The Political Philosophy of Needs*, Cambridge: Cambridge University Press, 2003.

——, 'Human Needs, Land Reform and the South African Constitution', *Politikon*, 33 (2) (2006), 133–145.

——, 'Collective Unfreedom in South Africa', *Contemporary Politics*, 17 (4) (2011), 355–372.

——, *Freedom is Power: Liberty Through Political Representation*, Cambridge: Cambridge University Press, 2014.

Hamilton, A., Madison, J. and Jay, J., *The Federalist*, T. Ball (ed.), Cambridge: Cambridge University Press, 2003 [1787].

Hamilton, J. and Flavin, M., 'On the Limitations of Government Borrowing: A Framework for Empirical Testing', *The American Economic Review*, 76 (4) (1986), 808–819.

Hamilton, L. and Viegi, N., 'Debt, Democracy and Representation in South Africa', *Representation*, 45 (2) (2009), 193–212.

Harvey, R., *The Fall of Apartheid: The Inside Story from Smuts to Mbeki*, 2nd Revised Edition, London: Palgrave, 2003.

Hayek, F. A., *The Constitution of Liberty*, London: Routledge, 1960.

Hayward, C., 'On Representation and Democratic Legitimacy', in Shapiro et al. (eds), *Political Representation*, Cambridge: Cambridge University Press, 2010, pp. 111–135.

Hegel, G. W. F., *Phenomenology of Spirit*, A. V. Miller (trans.), J. N. Findlay (foreword), Oxford: Oxford University Press, 1977 [1807].

Hirsch, A., *Season of Hope: Economic Reform Under Mandela and Mbeki*, Durban: University of KwaZulu-Natal Press, 2005.

Hobbes, T., *Leviathan*, R. Tuck (ed.), Cambridge: Cambridge University Press, 1996 [1651].

Holmes, S., *Passions and Constraint: On the Theory of Liberal Democracy*, Chicago and London: University of Chicago Press, 1995.

Hoogeveen, J. and Özler, B., 'Poverty and Inequality in Post-apartheid South Africa', in H. Bhorat and R. Kanbur (eds), *Poverty and Policy in Post-Apartheid South Africa*, Pretoria: HSRC Press, 2006.

Hunt, L., *Inventing Human Rights: A History*, New York: Norton, 2008.

Huntington, S., *The Third Wave: Democratization in the Late Twentieth Century*, Norman: University of Oklahoma Press, 1991.

Jefferson, T., *The Papers of Thomas Jefferson*, J. P. Boyd et al. (eds), Princeton: Princeton University Press, 1950.

Johnson, R. W., 'Mosiuoa "Terror" Lekota Threatens to Topple the ANC', *The Sunday Times* (19 October 2008).

Karis, T. and Carter, G. M., *From Protest to Challenge: A Documentary History of African Politics in South Africa, 1882–1964, Vol 2*, Stanford: Hoover Institution Press, 1973.

Kasrils, R., *Armed & Dangerous: From Undercover Struggle to Freedom*, Updated Edition, Johannebsurg: Jacana, 2013.

Keynes, J. M., *A Tract on Monetary Reform*, London: MacMillan and Co, 1923.

Klein, N., *The Shock Doctrine*, London: Penguin, 2007.

Klug, H., *Constituting Democracy: Law, Globalism and South Africa's Political Reconstruction*, Cambridge: Cambridge University Press, 2000.

Kramer, M. H., *The Quality of Freedom*, Oxford: Oxford University Press, 2003.

Leatt, A., Income Poverty in South Africa, 2006. Available from: http://www.ci.org.za/depts/ci/pubs/pdf/general/gauge2006/gauge2006_incomepoverty.pdf [accessed July 2010].

Lijphart, A., *The Politics of Accommodation: Pluralism and Democracy in the Netherlands*, Berkeley: University of California Press, 1975.

——, *Democracy in Plural Societies: A Comparative Exploration*, New Haven: Yale University Press, 1977.

Lindblom, C., 'The Market as Prison', *Journal of Politics*, 44 (2) (1982), 324–326.

Live, T., 'Cele points finger at "Nigerians in Sandton"', *Time Live* (7 December 2009).

Livy, T., *History of Rome from Its Foundation: Rome and the Mediterranean [Ab Urbe Condita]*, H. Bettenson (trans.), London: Penguin, 2005.

Locke, J., *Two Treatises on Government*, Cambridge: Cambridge University Press, 1988 [1689].

Lodge, T., *Politics in South Africa: From Mandela to Mbeki*, Cape Town: David Philip, 2002.

——, *Sharpeville: An Apartheid Massacre and Its Consequences*, Oxford: Oxford University Press, 2011.

Lovett, F., *A General Theory of Domination and Justice*, Cambridge: Cambridge University Press, 2010.

Lukes, S., *Power: A Radical View*, Second Edition, New York: Palgrave Macmillan, 2005.

Macdonald, J., *A Free Nation Deep in Debt: The Financial Roots of Democracy*,
    Princeton: Princeton University Press, 2006.
Machiavelli, N., *The Discourses*, B. Crick (ed.), L. J. Walker (trans.) with revisions by
    B. Richardson, London: Penguin, 2003, ca. 1517.
Macroeconomic Research Group, *Making Democracy Work: A Framework for
    Macroeconomic Policy in South Africa*, Cape Town: Centre for Development Studies,
    1993.
Mail & Guardian, 'SA Murder Rate Drops Slightly, Overall Crime Up', *Mail & Guardian*,
    22 September 2009.
Maitland, F. W., *State, Trust and Corporation*, D. Runciman and M. Ryan (eds),
    Cambridge: Cambridge University Press, 2003.
Mandela, N., *Long Walk to Freedom: The Autobiography of Nelson Mandela*,
    Johannesburg: Macdonald Purnell, 1995.
Manin, B., *The Principles of Representative Government*, Cambridge: Cambridge
    University Press, 1997.
Marrian, N., 'Mashatile Wants Constituencies for MPs', *Business Day*, (25 July 2013),. 3.
Marx, K., 'On the Jewish Question', in K. Marx, *Early Political Writings*, J. O'Malley and
    R. A. Davis (eds), Cambridge: Cambridge University Press, 1994 [1843].
——, *The Communist Manifesto*, introduced G. Stedman-Jones, London: Penguin,
    2002 [1848].
Marx, K. and Engels, F., *The German Ideology in Marx Engels Collected Works in Marx
    Engels Collected Works*, Vol 5, London: Lawrence and Wishart, 1976, ca. 1846.
Mattes, R., 'Democracy Without People: Political Institutions and Citizenship in the
    New South Africa', *Afrobarometer Working Paper No. 82* (November 2007), Cape
    Town: Institute for Democracy in South Africa (IDASA).
Mbeki, T., 'Questions that Demand an Answer', ANC Today, 4 (36) (2004), http://www.
    anc.org.za/docs/anctoday/2004/at36.htm.
McCormick, J. P., *Machiavellian Democracy*, Cambridge: Cambridge University Press,
    2011.
Metcalfe, M., 'Mistakes We Cannot Make Again', *Mail & Guardian*, (3–9 September
    2010).
Meth, C., 'Half-measures Revisited: The ANC's Unemployment and Poverty Reduction
    Goals', in H. Bhorat and R. Kanbur (eds), *Poverty and Policy in Post-Apartheid South
    Africa*, Cape Town: HSRC Press, 2006.
Michie, J. and Padayachee, V., 'Three Years After Apartheid: Growth, Employment and
    Redistribution?', *Cambridge Journal of Economics*, 22 (1998), 623–635.
Mill, J. S., *On Liberty and Other Essays*, John Gray (ed.), Oxford: Oxford University
    Press, 2008 [1859].
Mngxitama, A., 'Tripartite Tussle? Get Real, It's Just a Game', *Mail & Guardian*,
    (3–9 September 2010).
Montesquieu, Cd.e., *The Spirit of the Laws*, A. M. Cohler, B. C. Miller and H. S. Stone
    (eds), Cambridge: Cambridge University Press, 1989 [1748].

Mosley, L., 'Constraints, Opportunities and Information: Financial Market-
Government Relations Around the World', in P. Bardhan, S. Bowles. and
E. Wallerstein (eds), *Globalization and Egalitarian Redistribution*, Princeton, NJ:
Princeton University Press, 2006.

Mouffe, C., *The Democratic Paradox*, London: Verso, 2000.

Munusamy, R., 'Cyril Ramaphosa: Betrayal Does Not Get More Painful Than This',
The Guardian, 25 October 2012. Available from: www.guardian.co.uk/world/2012/
oct/25/cyril-ramaphosa-marikana-email [accessed 25 October 2012].

Nattrass, N., 'Politics and Economics in ANC Economic Policy', *African Affairs*,
93 (1994), 343–359.

——, 'AIDS and Human Security in Southern Africa', *Social Dynamics*, 28 (1) (2002),
1–19.

Netshitenzhe, J., 'The National Democratic Revolution: Is it Still on Track?', *Umrabulo*,
1 (4th Quarter, 1996), Available from: http://www.anc.org.za/show.php?id=2968
[accessed 21 July 2010].

Nietzsche, F., 'Notebook 34, April–June 1885' 34[250] and 'Notebook I, Autumn 1885–
Spring 1886' I[33]', in R. Bittner (ed.), *Writings from the Late Notebooks*, Cambridge:
Cambridge University Press, 2003.

North, D. C. and Weingast, B. R., 'Constitutions and Commitment: The Evolution of
Institutions Governing Public Choice in Seventeenth Century England', *Journal of
Economic History*, 49 (4) (1989), 803–832.

Padayachee, V. and Sherbut, G., 'Ideas and Power: Academic Economists and the
Making of Economic policy', in W. Gumede and L. Dikeni (eds), *South African
Democracy and the Retreat of Intellectuals*, Johannesburg: Jacana Media, 2009.

Persson, T. and Tabellini, G., 'Is Inequality Harmful for Growth? Theory and Evidence',
American Economic Review, 84 (3) (1994), 600–621.

Pettit, P., *Republicanism: A Theory of Freedom and Government*, Oxford: Clarendon
Press, 1997.

——, *On The People's Terms*, Cambridge: Cambridge University Press, 2012.

Pickwoth, E., 'Joint Initiative to Foster Education Reform', *Business Day* (2 August
2013), 4.

Piper, L., *Theorizing Democracy in Local Government in South Africa*, UKZN, Durban:
unpublished paper presented at Politics Seminar, November 2005.

Piper, L., Barichievy, K. and Parker, B., 'Assessing "Participatory Governance" in Local
Government: A Case-study of Two South African Cities', *Politeia*, 24 (3) (2005),
370–393.

Pitkin, H. F., *The Concept of Representation*, Berkeley, CA, Los Angeles, CA and London:
University of California Press, 1967.

——, 'Representation', in T. Ball, J. Farr and R. L. Hanson (eds) *Political Innovation
and Conceptual Change*, Cambridge: Cambridge University Press, 1989, pp. 132–154.

Poverty Net, Understanding Poverty and World Bank Poverty Report (2008). Available
from: http://web.worldbank.org/WBSITE/EXTERNAL/TOPICS/EXTPOVERTY/

EXTPA/0,contentMDK:20153855~menuPK:435040~pagePK:148956~piPK:216618~
theSitePK:430367,00.html [accessed 10 July 2010].

Przeworski, A., Stokes, S. and Manin, B., *Democracy, Accountability and Representation*,
Cambridge: Cambridge University Press, 1999.

Rawls, J., *A Theory of Justice*, Cambridge, MA: Harvard University Press, 1971.

——, *Political Liberalism*, New York: Columbia University Press, 1996.

Rehfeld, A., *The Concept of Constituency: Political Representation, Democratic
Legitimacy, and Institutional Design*, Cambridge: Cambridge University Press, 2005.

Rosanvallon, P., *Le Sacre du citoyen: Histoire du suffrage universel en France*, Paris:
Gallimard, 1992.

Rousseau, J.-J., 'The Social Contract', in V. Gourevitch (ed.), *The Social Contract and
Other Later Political Writings*, Cambridge: Cambridge University Press, 1997 [1762].

Schattschneider, E. E., *Party Government*, New York: Farrar and Rinehart, 1942.

Schumpeter, J., *Capitalism, Socialism, and Democracy*, New York: Harper, 1942.

Seekings, J., 'Poverty and Inequality in South Africa, 1994–2007', in I. Shapiro and
K. Trebeau (eds), *After Apartheid: Reinventing South Africa?*, Charlottesville and
London: University of Virginia Press, 2011.

Seekings, J., Nattras, N. and Leibbrandt, M., 'Income Inequality After Apartheid', *CSSR
Working Paper No. 75* (2004), Centre for Social Science Research, University of Cape
Town.

Sen, A., *Collective Choice and Social Welfare*, San Francisco: Holden Day, 1970.

——, *Poverty and Famines: An Essay on Entitlement and Deprivation*, Oxford:
Clarendon Press, 1981.

——, *Commodities and Capabilities*, Amsterdam: North-Holland, 1985a.

——, 'Well-being, Agency and Freedom: The Dewey Lectures 1984', *Journal of
Philosophy*, 82 (4) (1985b), pp. 169–221.

——, 'The Equality of What?', in S. M. McMurrin (ed.), *Liberty, Equality, and Law*,
Cambridge: Cambridge University Press, 1987a, pp. 136–162.

——, *On Ethics and Economics*, Oxford: Basil Blackwell, 1987b.

——, *Inequality Reexamined*, Oxford: Basil Clarendon Press, 1992.

——, 'Positional Objectivity', in *Philosophy and Public Affairs*, 22 (1992), pp. 126–145.

——, *Development as Freedom*, Oxford: Oxford University Press, 1999.

Shapiro, I., *The State of Democratic Theory*, Princeton: Princeton University Press, 2003.

Shapiro, I. and Kymlicka, W. (eds), *Ethnicity and Group Rights: NOMOS XXXIX*, New
York: New York University Press, 1997.

Shapiro, I., Stokes, S. C., Wood, E. J. and Kirshner, A. S., *Political Representation*,
Cambridge: Cambridge University Press, 2010.

Shapiro, I. and Tebeau, K., *After Apartheid: Reinventing South Africa?*, Charlottesville
and London: University of Virginia Press, 2011.

Sieyès, E. J., *Political Writings*, M. Sonenscher (ed.), Indianapolis/Cambridge: Hackett,
2003 [1789].

Skinner, Q., 'Machiavelli's *Discorsi* and the Pre-humanist Origins of Republican Ideas', in
    G. Bock, Q. Skinner and M. Viroli (eds), *Machiavelli and Republicanism*, Cambridge:
    Cambridge University Press, 1991, pp. 121–142.
——, 'The Idea of Negative Liberty', in R. Rorty, J. B. Schneewind and Q. Skinner
    (eds), *Philosophy in History*, Cambridge: Cambridge University Press, 1984.
——, *Liberty Before Liberalism*, Cambridge: Cambridge University Press, 1998.
——, 'The Idea of Negative Liberty: Machiavellian and Modern Perspectives', in *Vision
    of Politics Vol II Renaissance Virtues*, Cambridge: Cambridge University Press, 2002,
    pp. 186–212.
——, *Hobbes and Republican Liberty*, Cambridge: Cambridge University Press, 2008.
Slovo, J., 'Negotiations: What Room for Compromise' (mimeo).
Smith, D., 'Lonmin Emails Paint ANC Elder as a Born-again Robber Baron',
    The Guardian, 24 October 2012. Available from: www.guardian.co.uk/world/2012/
    oct/2/lonmin-emails-anc-elder-baron [accessed 25 October 2012].
Sonenscher, M., 'Introduction', in E. J. Sieyès, *Political Writings*, M. Sonenscher (ed.),
    Indianapolis/Cambridge: Hackett, 2003.
South African Institute of Race Relations, 'Unemployment and Poverty: An Overview
    28th November 2008'. Available from: http://www.sairr.org.za/sairr-today/news_
    item.2008-11-28.9488661622/?searchterm=poverty%20statistics [accessed 5 July
    2010].
South African Police Service, 'South African Government Crime Statistics 2009'.
    Available from: http://www.saps.gov.za/statistics/reports/crimestats/2009/crime_
    stats.htm [accessed 5 July 2010].
——, 'Address by Minister of Police, Nathi Mthethwa, Deputy Minister Fikile Mbalula
    and Police Commissioner Bheki Cele to the members of the National Press Club'.
    Available from: http://www.saps.gov.za/_dynamicModules/internetSite/newsBuild.
    asp?myURL=938 [accessed 15 July 2010).
Sparks, A., *Tomorrow is Another Country: The Inside Story of South Africa's Road to
    Change*, Pretoria: Struik, 1994.
Spitz, R. and Chaskalson, M., *The Politics of a Transition: A Hidden History of South
    Africa's Negotiated Settlement*, Oxford: Hart, 2000.
Star, T., 'Still Too Many Murders': Experts Voice Caution as Major-crime Stats Show
    Decline', *The Star* (10 September 2010).
Stasavage, D., *Public Debt and the Birth of the Democratic State: France and Great
    Britain, 1688–1789*, Cambridge: Cambridge University Press, 2003.
Statistics South Africa (SSA), 'General Household Survey July 2008', 2009. Available
    from: http://www.statssa.gov.za/publications/P0318/P0318July2008.pdf [accessed
    8 July 2010].
——, 'Quarterly Labour Force Survey Quarter 4, 2009', 2010a. Available from: http://
    www.statssa.gov.za/publications/P0211/P02114thQuarter2009.pdf [accessed 12 July
    2010].

——, 'General Household Survey 2010 (Revised Version)', *Statistics Release PO318*, Pretoria: Statistics South Africa, 2010b.

——, 'Census: Statistical Release (Revised)', P0301.4, 2011. Available from: http://www.statssa.gov.za/publications/P03014/P030142011.pdf [accessed on 25 May 2013].

——, 'General Household Survey 2012 (Revised Version)', Statistics Release *PO318* 2013. Available from: http://www.statssa.gov.za/Publications/P0318/P0318August2012.pdf [accessed 28 August 2013].

——, 'Quarterly Labour Force Survey: Quarter 1, 2013', Statistical Release P0211, 2013. Available from: http://www.statssa.gov.za/publications/P0211/P02111stQuarter2013.pdf [accessed on 28 August 2013].

——, ' 2007/2008 Human Development Report, South Africa', 2008. Available from: http://hdrstats.undp.org/countries/country_fact_sheets/cty_fs_ZAF.html [accessed 9 July 2010].

——, 'Income and Expenditure of Households 2005/2006', 2009. Available from: http://www.statssa.gov.za/publications/P0100/P01002005.pdf [accessed on 3 October 2013].

Steiner, H., 'Essay on Rights', *Canadian Journal of Philosophy*, 26 (2) (June 1996).

——, 'Individual Liberty', in D. Miller (ed.), *The Liberty Reader*, Edinburgh: Edinburgh University Press, 2006, 123–140.

Stiglitz, J., *Making Globalization Work*, London: Penguin, 2007.

Suttner, R., 'Democratic Transition and Consolidation in South Africa: The Advice of "the Experts"', *Current Sociology*, 52 (5) (2004), 755–773.

Tapscott, C., 'The Challenges of Building Participatory Government' in L. Thompson (ed.), *Participatory Governance: Citizens and the State in South Africa*, University of the Western Cape, 2007, published by African Centre for Citizenship and Democracy, Cape Town: University of the Western Cape (2007). Available from: http://www.drc-citizenship.org/system/assets/1052734741/original/1052734741-thompson.2007-participatory.pdf?1305365928, pp. 81-95.

Taylor, C., 'What's Wrong with Negative Liberty', in A. Ryan (ed.), *The Idea of Freedom*, Oxford: Oxford University Press, 1979, 175–193.

Terreblanche, S., *Lost in Transformation: South Africa's Search for a New Future Since 1986*, Johannesburg: KMM Review Publishing, 2012.

The Forum for Public Dialogue (FPD), 'Electoral Systems and Accountability: Comparative Case Studies and Lessons for South Africa', Working Paper Draft (23 July 2013), 46–48.

The Presidency Republic of South Africa, Development Indicators 2008 (2008). Available from: http://www.info.gov.za/view/DownloadFileAction?id=84952 [accessed 9 July 2010].

Thorn, H., *Anti-Apartheid and the Emergence of a Global Civil Society*, Basingstoke: Palgrave Macmillan, 2009.

Tsebelis, G., *Veto Players: How Political Institutions Work*, Princeton: Princeton University Press, 2002.

Tsoeu-Ntokoane, S., 'The Politics of Constitutionalism in South Africa: Institutions Supporting Democracy', unpublished University of Johannesburg DPhil Thesis.

Turok, B., *From the Freedom Charter to Polokwane: The Evolution of ANC Economic Policy*, Cape Town: New Agenda: South African Journal of Social and Economic Policy, 2008.

United Nations Development Programme (UNDP), *Human Development Report 1999*, Geneva: United Nations Development Programme, 1999.

———, *Human Development Report 2013: The Rise of the South: Human Progress in a Diverse World*, Geneva: United Nations Development Programme, 2013a. Available from: http://hdr.undp.org/en/media/HDR_2013_EN_complete.pdf [accessed on 23 August 2013].

———, *Human Development Report 2013: The Rise of the South: Human Progress in a Diverse World: Explanatory Note on 2013 HDI CompositeIndices: South Africa*, Geneva: United Nations Development Programme, 2013b. Available from: http://hdrstats.undp.org/images/explanations/ZAF.pdf [accessed 26 August 2013].

United Nations, *Human Development Report 2002: Deepening Democracy in a Fragmented World*, Oxford: Oxford University Press, 2002.

Urbinati, N., *Representative Democracy: Principles and Genealogy*, Chicago: Chicago University Press, 2008.

Van der Walt, A. J., 'Property Rights, Land Rights, and Environmental Rights', in Van Wyk et al. (eds), *Rights and Constitutionalism: The New South African Legal Order*, Oxford: Clarendon Press, 1996, pp. 455–501.

Vieira, M. B. and Runciman, D., *Representation*, Cambridge: Polity Press, 2008.

Waldron, J., *Law and Disagreement*, Oxford: Oxford University Press, 1999a.

———, *The Dignity of Legislation*, Cambridge: Cambridge University Press, 1999b.

Weingast, B., 'The Political Foundations of Limited Government: Parliament and Sovereign Debt in 17th and 18th Century England', in J. Drobak and J. Nye (eds), *Frontiers of the New Institutional Economics*, London: Harcourt Brace, 1997, 213–246.

Weymans, W., 'Freedom Through Political Representation: Lefort, Gauchet and Rosanvallon on the Relationship Between State and Society', *European Journal of Political Theory*, 4 (3) (2005), 263–282.

Wilkinson, R. G., *Unhealthy Societies: The Afflictions of Inequality*, London: Routledge, 1996.

———, *The Impact of Inequality: How to Make Sick Societies Healthier*, London: Routledge, 2005.

Wilkinson, R. G. and Pickett, K., *The Spirit Level: Why More Equal Societies Almost All Do Better*, London: Allen Lane, 2009.

Wirszubski, Ch., *Libertas as a Political Idea at Rome During the Late Republic and Early Principate*, Cambridge: Cambridge University Press, 1968.

Wolin, S. S., 'Fugitive Democracy', in S. Benhabib (ed.), *Democracy and Difference*,
    Princeton: Princeton University Press, 1996.
World Bank, *The East Asian Miracle*, Oxford: Oxford University Press, 1993.
——, '2013 People: World Development Indicators: Distribution of Income or
    Consumption' (2013). Available from: http://wdi.worldbank.org/table/2.9 [accessed
    on 27 August 2013].
Young, M., *Inclusion and Democracy*, Oxford: Oxford University Press, 2000.

Index